THE GOSPEL OF MARK

THE IGNATIUS CATHOLIC STUDY BIBLE

REVISED STANDARD VERSION
SECOND CATHOLIC EDITION

THE GOSPEL OF MARK

With Introduction, Commentary, and Notes

by

Scott Hahn and Curtis Mitch

and

with Study Questions by

Dennis Walters

IGNATIUS PRESS   SAN FRANCISCO

Published with ecclesiastical approval.

Original RSV Bible text:
Nihil obstat: Thomas Hanlon, S.T.L., L.S.S, Ph.L.
Imprimatur: +Peter W. Bertholome, D.D.
Bishop of Saint Cloud, Minnesota
May 11, 1966

Second Catholic Edition approved under the same *imprimatur* by the
Secretariat for Doctrine and Pastoral Practices,
National Conference of Catholic Bishops
February 29, 2001

Introduction, commentaries, and notes:
Nihil obstat: Rev. Msgr. J. Warren Holleran, S.T.D.
Imprimatur: + William J. Levada,
Archbishop of San Francisco,
January 22, 2001

Second Catholic Edition approved by the
National Council of the Churches of Christ in the USA

Cover art: *Saint Mark*,
Antonio Triva (ca. 1626–1699), S. Maria della Salute, Venice
Cameraphoto/Art Resource, New York

Cover design by Riz Boncan Marsella

Published for Ignatius Press in 2001 by
Thomas Nelson Publishers, Nashville, Tennessee
Bible text: Revised Standard Version, Second Catholic Edition
© 2001 by the Division of Christian Education of the
National Council of the Churches of Christ in the United States of America
All rights reserved

Introductions, commentaries, notes, headings, and study questions
© 2001, Ignatius Press, San Francisco
All rights reserved
ISBN 0–89870–818–4
Printed in the United States of America ∞

CONTENTS

INTRODUCTION TO THE IGNATIUS STUDY BIBLE

You are approaching the "word of God". This is the title Christians most commonly give to the Bible, and the expression is rich in meaning. It is also the title given to the Second Person of the Blessed Trinity, God the Son. For Jesus Christ became flesh for our salvation, and "the name by which he is called is The Word of God" (Rev 19:13; cf. Jn 1:14).

The word of God is Scripture. The Word of God is Jesus. This close association between God's *written* word and his *eternal* Word is intentional and has been the custom of the Church since the first generation. "All Sacred Scripture is but one book, and this one book is Christ, 'because all divine Scripture speaks of Christ, and all divine Scripture is fulfilled in Christ'[1]" (CCC 134). This does not mean that the Scriptures are divine in the same way that Jesus is divine. They are, rather, divinely inspired and, as such, are unique in world literature, just as the Incarnation of the eternal Word is unique in human history.

Yet we can say that the inspired word resembles the incarnate Word in several important ways. Jesus Christ is the Word of God incarnate. In his humanity, he is like us in all things, except for sin. As a work of man, the Bible is like any other book, except without error. Both Christ and Scripture, says the Second Vatican Council, are given "for the sake of our salvation" (*Dei Verbum* 11), and both give us God's definitive revelation of himself. We cannot, therefore, conceive of one without the other: the Bible without Jesus, or Jesus without the Bible. Each is the interpretive key to the other. And because Christ is the subject of all the Scriptures, St. Jerome insists, "Ignorance of the Scriptures is ignorance of Christ"[2] (CCC 133).

When we approach the Bible, then, we approach Jesus, the Word of God; and in order to encounter Jesus, we must approach him in a prayerful study of the inspired word of God, the Sacred Scriptures.

Inspiration and Inerrancy   The Catholic Church makes mighty claims for the Bible, and our acceptance of those claims is essential if we are to read the Scriptures and apply them to our lives as the Church intends. So it is not enough merely to nod at words like "inspired", "unique", or "inerrant". We have to understand what the Church means by these terms, and we have to make that understanding our own. After all, what we believe about the Bible will inevitably influence the way we read the Bible. The way we read the Bible, in turn, will determine what we "get out" of its sacred pages.

These principles hold true no matter what we read: a news report, a search warrant, an advertisement, a paycheck, a doctor's prescription, an eviction notice. How (or whether) we read these things depends largely upon our preconceived notions about the reliability and authority of their sources—and the potential they have for affecting our lives. In some cases, to misunderstand a document's authority can lead to dire consequences. In others, it can keep us from enjoying rewards that are rightfully ours. In the case of the Bible, both the rewards and the consequences involved take on an ultimate value.

What does the Church mean, then, when she affirms the words of St. Paul: "All scripture is inspired by God" (2 Tim 3:16)? Since the term "inspired" in this passage could be translated "God-breathed", it follows that God breathed forth his word in the Scriptures as you and I breathe forth air when we speak. This means that God is the primary author of the Bible. He certainly employed human authors in this task as well, but he did not merely assist them while they wrote or subsequently approve what they had written. God the Holy Spirit is the *principal* author of Scripture, while the human writers are *instrumental* authors. These human authors freely wrote everything, and only those things, that God wanted: the word of God in the very words of God. This miracle of dual authorship extends to the whole of Scripture, and to every one of its parts, so that whatever the human authors affirm, God likewise affirms through their words.

The principle of biblical inerrancy follows logically from this principle of divine authorship. After all, God cannot lie, and he cannot make mistakes. Since the Bible is divinely inspired, it must be without error in everything that its divine and human authors affirm to be true. This means that biblical inerrancy is a mystery even broader in scope than infallibility, which guarantees for us that the Church will always teach the truth concerning faith and morals. Of course the mantle of inerrancy likewise covers faith and morals, but it extends even farther to ensure that all the facts and events of salvation history are accurately presented for us in the Scriptures. Inerrancy is our guarantee that the words and deeds of God found in the Bible are unified and true, declaring with one voice the wonders of his saving love.

[1] Hugh of St. Victor, *De arca Noe* 2, 8: PL 176, 642: cf. ibid. 2, 9: PL 176, 642–43.
[2] *DV* 25; cf. Phil 3:8 and St. Jerome, *Commentariorum Isaiam libri xviii*, prol.: PL 24, 17b.

The guarantee of inerrancy does not mean, however, that the Bible is an all-purpose encyclopedia of information covering every field of study. The Bible is not, for example, a textbook in the empirical sciences, and it should not be treated as one. When biblical authors relate facts of the natural order, we can be sure they are speaking in a purely descriptive and "phenomenological" way, according to the way things appeared to their senses.

Biblical Authority Implicit in these doctrines is God's desire to make himself known to the world and to enter a loving relationship with every man, woman, and child he has created. God gave us the Scriptures not just to inform or motivate us; more than anything he wants to save us. This higher purpose underlies every page of the Bible, indeed every word of it.

In order to reveal himself, God used what theologians call "accommodation". Sometimes the Lord stoops down to communicate by "condescension"— that is, he speaks as humans speak, as if he had the same passions and weakness that we do (for example, God says he was "sorry" that he made man in Genesis 6:6). Other times he communicates by "elevation"—that is, by endowing human words with divine power (for example, through the prophets). The numerous examples of divine accommodation in the Bible are an expression of God's wise and fatherly ways. For a sensitive father can speak with his children either by condescension, as in baby talk, or by elevation, by bringing a child's understanding up to a more mature level.

God's word is thus saving, fatherly, and personal. Because it speaks directly to us, we must never be indifferent to its content; after all, the word of God is at once the object, cause, and support of our faith. It is, in fact, a test of our faith, since we see in the Scriptures only what faith disposes us to see. If we believe what the Church believes, we will see in Scripture the saving, inerrant, and divinely authored revelation of the Father. If we believe otherwise, we see another book altogether.

This test applies not only to rank-and-file believers but also to the Church's theologians and hierarchy, and even the Magisterium. Vatican II stressed in recent times that Scripture must be "the very soul of sacred theology" (*Dei Verbum* 24). Joseph Cardinal Ratzinger echoes this powerful teaching with his own, insisting that, "The *normative theologians* are the authors of Holy Scripture" [emphasis added]. Elsewhere he reminds us that Scripture and the Church's dogmatic teaching are tied tightly together, to the point of being inseparable. He states: "Dogma is by definition nothing other than an interpretation of Scripture." The defined dogmas of our faith, then, encapsulate the Church's infallible interpretation of Scripture, and theology is a further reflection upon that work.

The Senses of Scripture Because the Bible has both divine and human authors, we are required to master a different sort of reading than we are used to. First, we must read Scripture according to its *literal* sense, as we read any other human literature. At this initial stage, we strive to discover the meaning of the words and expressions used by the biblical writers as they were understood in their original setting and by their original recipients. This means, among other things, that we do not interpret everything we read "literalistically", as though Scripture never speaks in a figurative or symbolic way (it often does!). Rather, we read it according to the rules that govern its different literary forms of writing, depending on whether we are reading a narrative, a poem, a letter, a parable, or an apocalyptic vision. The Church calls us to read the divine books in this way to ensure that we understand what the human authors were laboring to explain to God's people.

The literal sense, however, is not the only sense of Scripture, since we interpret its sacred pages according to the *spiritual* senses as well. In this way, we search out what the Holy Spirit is trying to tell us, beyond even what the human authors have consciously asserted. Whereas the literal sense of Scripture describes a historical reality—a fact, precept, or event—the spiritual senses disclose deeper mysteries revealed through the historical realities. What the soul is to the body, the spiritual senses are to the literal. You can distinguish them; but if you try to separate them, death immediately follows. St. Paul was the first to insist upon this and warn of its consequences: "God ... has qualified us to be ministers of a new covenant, not in a written code but in the Spirit; for the written code kills, but the Spirit gives life" (2 Cor 3:5–6).

Catholic tradition recognizes three spiritual senses that stand upon the foundation of the literal sense of Scripture (see CCC 115). (1) The first is the *allegorical* sense, which unveils the spiritual and prophetic meaning of biblical history. Allegorical interpretations thus reveal how persons, events, and institutions of Scripture can point beyond themselves toward greater mysteries yet to come (OT), or display the fruits of mysteries already revealed (NT). Christians have often read the Old Testament in this way to discover how the mystery of Christ in the New Covenant was once hidden in the Old, and how the full significance of the Old Covenant was finally made manifest in the New. Allegorical significance is likewise latent in the New Testament, especially in the life and deeds of Jesus recorded in the Gospels. Because Christ is the Head of the Church and the source of her spiritual life, what was accomplished in Christ the Head during his earthly life prefigures what he continually produces in his members through grace. The allegorical sense builds up the virtue of faith. (2) The second is the *tropological* or *moral* sense, which reveals how the actions of God's people in the Old Testament and the life of Jesus in the New Testament prompt us to form virtuous habits in our own lives. It therefore draws from Scripture warnings against sin and vice, as well as inspirations to pursue holiness and purity. The moral sense is intended to build up the virtue of charity. (3) The third is the *anagogical* sense, which points upward to heavenly glory. It shows us how countless events in the Bible prefigure our final union with God in eternity, and how things that are "seen" on earth are figures of things "unseen" in heaven. Because the anagogical sense leads us to contemplate our destiny, it is meant to build up the virtue of hope. Together with the literal sense, then, these spiritual senses draw out the fullness of what God wants to give us through his Word and as such comprise what ancient tradition has called the "full sense" of Sacred Scripture.

All of this means that the deeds and events of the Bible are charged with meaning beyond what is immediately apparent to the reader. In essence, that meaning is Jesus Christ and the salvation he died to give us. This is especially true of the books of the New Testament, which proclaim Jesus explicitly; but it is also true of the Old Testament, which speaks of Jesus in more hidden and symbolic ways. The human authors of the Old Testament told us as much as they were able, but they could not clearly discern the shape of all future events standing at such a distance. It is the Bible's divine Author, the Holy Spirit, who could and did foretell the saving work of Christ, from the first page of the Book of Genesis onward.

The New Testament did not, therefore, abolish the Old. Rather, the New fulfilled the Old, and in doing so, it lifted the veil that kept hidden the face of the Lord's bride. Once the veil is removed, we suddenly see the world of the Old Covenant charged with grandeur. Water, fire, clouds, gardens, trees, hills, doves, lambs—all of these things are memorable details in the history and poetry of Israel. But now, seen in the light of Jesus Christ, they are much more. For the Christian with eyes to see, water symbolizes the saving power of Baptism; fire, the Holy Spirit; the spotless lamb, Christ crucified; Jerusalem, the city of heavenly glory.

The spiritual reading of Scripture is nothing new. Indeed the very first Christians read the Bible this way. St. Paul describes Adam as a "type" that prefigured Jesus Christ (Rom 5:14). A "type" is a real person, place, thing, or event in the Old Testament that foreshadows something greater in the New. From this term we get the word "typology", referring to the study of how the Old Testament prefigures Christ (CCC 128–30). Elsewhere St. Paul draws deeper meanings out of the story of Abraham's sons, declaring, "This is an allegory" (Gal 4:24). He is not suggesting that these events of the distant past never really happened; he is saying

that the events both happened *and* signified something more glorious yet to come.

The New Testament later describes the Tabernacle of ancient Israel as "a copy and shadow of the heavenly sanctuary" (Heb 8:5) and the Mosaic Law as a "shadow of the good things to come" (Heb 10:1). St. Peter, in turn, notes that Noah and his family were "saved through water" in a way that "corresponds" to sacramental Baptism, which "now saves you" (1 Pet 3:20–21). Interestingly, the expression that is translated "corresponds" in this verse is a Greek term that denotes the fulfillment or counterpart of an ancient "type".

We need not look to the apostles, however, to justify a spiritual reading of the Bible. After all, Jesus himself read the Old Testament this way. He referred to Jonah (Mt 12:39), Solomon (Mt 12:42), the Temple (Jn 2:19), and the brazen serpent (Jn 3:14) as "signs" that pointed forward to him. We see in Luke's Gospel, as Christ comforted the disciples on the road to Emmaus, that "beginning with Moses and all the prophets, he interpreted to them in all the scriptures the things concerning himself" (Lk 24:27). It was precisely this extensive spiritual interpretation of the Old Testament that made such an impact on these once-discouraged travelers, causing their hearts to "burn" within them (Lk 24:32).

Criteria for Biblical Interpretation. We too must learn to discern the "full sense" of Scripture as it includes both the literal and spiritual senses together. Still, this does not mean we should "read into" the Bible meanings that are not really there. Spiritual exegesis is not an unrestrained flight of the imagination. Rather, it is a sacred science that proceeds according to certain principles and stands accountable to sacred tradition, the Magisterium, and the wider community of biblical interpreters (both living and deceased).

In searching out the full sense of a text, we should always avoid the extreme tendency to "over-spiritualize" in a way that minimizes or denies the Bible's literal truth. St. Thomas Aquinas was well aware of this danger and asserted that "all other senses of Sacred Scripture are based on the literal" (*STh* I, 1, 10, *ad* 1, quoted in CCC 116). On the other hand, we should never confine the meaning of a text to the literal, intended sense of its human author, as if the divine Author did not intend the passage to be read in the light of Christ's coming.

Fortunately the Church has given us guidelines in our study of Scripture. The unique character and divine authorship of the Bible calls us to read it "in the Spirit" (*Dei Verbum* 12). Vatican II outlines this teaching in a practical way by directing us to read the Scriptures according to three specific criteria:

1. We must "[b]e especially attentive 'to the content and unity of the whole Scripture' " (CCC 112).

2. We must "[r]ead the Scripture within 'the living Tradition of the whole Church' " (CCC 113).

3. We must "[b]e attentive to the analogy of faith" (CCC 114; cf. Rom 12:6).

These criteria protect us from many of the dangers that ensnare readers of the Bible, from the newest inquirer to the most prestigious scholar. Reading Scripture out of context is one such pitfall, and probably the one most difficult to avoid. A memorable cartoon from the 1950s shows a young man poring over the pages of the Bible. He says to his sister: "Don't bother me now; I'm trying to find a Scripture verse to back up one of my preconceived notions." No doubt a biblical text pried from its context can be twisted to say something very different from what its author actually intended.

The Church's criteria guide us here by defining what constitutes the authentic "context" of a given biblical passage. The first criterion directs us to the literary context of every verse, including not only the words and paragraphs that surround it, but also the entire corpus of the biblical author's writings and, indeed, the span of the entire Bible. The *complete* literary context of any Scripture verse includes every text from Genesis to Revelation—because the Bible is a unified book, not just a library of different books. When the Church canonized the Book of Revelation, for example, she recognized it to be incomprehensible apart from the wider context of the entire Bible.

The second criterion places the Bible firmly within the context of a community that treasures a "living tradition". That community is the People of God down through the ages. Christians lived out their faith for well over a millennium before the printing press was invented. For centuries, few believers owned copies of the Gospels, and few people could read anyway. Yet they absorbed the gospel—through the sermons of their bishops and clergy, through prayer and meditation, through Christian art, through liturgical celebrations, and through oral tradition. These were expressions of the one "living tradition", a culture of living faith that stretches from ancient Israel to the contemporary Church. For the early Christians, the gospel could not be understood apart from that tradition. So it is with us. Reverence for the Church's tradition is what protects us from any sort of chronological or cultural provincialism, such as scholarly fads that arise and carry away a generation of interpreters before being dismissed by the next generation.

The third criterion places scriptural texts within the framework of faith. If we believe that the Scriptures are divinely inspired, we must also believe them to be internally coherent and consistent with all the doctrines that Christians believe. Remember, the Church's dogmas (such as the Real Presence, the papacy, the Immaculate Conception) are not something *added* to Scripture, but are the Church's infallible interpretation *of* Scripture.

Using This Study Guide This volume is designed to lead the reader through Scripture according to the Church's guidelines—faithful to the canon, to the tradition, and to the creeds. The Church's interpretive principles have thus shaped the component parts of this book, and they are designed to make the reader's study as effective and rewarding as possible.

Introductions: We have introduced the biblical book with an essay covering issues such as authorship, date of composition, purpose, and leading themes. This background information will assist readers to approach and understand the text on its own terms.

Annotations: The basic notes at the bottom of every page help the user to read the Scriptures with understanding. They by no means exhaust the meaning of the sacred text but provide background material to help the reader make sense of what he reads. Often these notes make explicit what the sacred writers assumed or held to be implicit. They also provide scores of historical, cultural, geographical, and theological information pertinent to the inspired narratives—information that can help the reader bridge the distance between the biblical world and his own.

Cross-References: Between the biblical text at the top of each page and the annotations at the bottom, numerous references are listed to point readers to other scriptural passages related to the one being studied. This follow-up is an essential part of any serious study. It is also an excellent way to discover how the content of Scripture "hangs together" in a providential unity. Along with biblical cross-references, the annotations refer to select paragraphs from the *Catechism of the Catholic Church*. These are not doctrinal "proof texts" but are designed to help the reader interpret the Bible in accordance with the mind of the Church. The *Catechism* references listed either handle the biblical text directly or treat a broader doctrinal theme that sheds significant light on that text.

Topical Essays, Word Studies, Charts: These features bring readers to a deeper understanding of select details. The *topical essays* take up major themes and explain them more thoroughly and theologically than the annotations, often relating them to the doctrines of the Church. Occasionally the annotations are supplemented by *word studies* that put readers in touch with the ancient languages of Scripture. These should help readers to understand better and appreciate the inspired terminology that runs throughout the sacred books. Also included are various *charts* that summarize biblical information "at a glance".

Icon Annotations: Three distinctive icons are

interspersed throughout the annotations, each one corresponding to one of the Church's three criteria for biblical interpretation. Bullets indicate the passage or passages to which these icons apply.

Notes marked by the book icon relate to the "content and unity" of Scripture, showing how particular passages of the Old Testament illuminate the mysteries of the New. Much of the information in these notes explains the original context of the citations and indicates how and why this has a direct bearing on Christ or the Church. Through these notes, the reader can develop a sensitivity to the beauty and unity of God's saving plan as it stretches across both Testaments.

Notes marked by the dove icon examine particular passages in light of the Church's "living tradition". Because the Holy Spirit both guides the Magisterium and inspires the spiritual senses of Scripture, these annotations supply information along both of these lines. On the one hand, they refer to the Church's doctrinal teaching as presented by various popes, creeds, and ecumenical councils; on the other, they draw from (and paraphrase) the spiritual interpretations of various Fathers, Doctors, and saints.

Notes marked by the key icon pertain to the "analogy of faith". Here we spell out how the mysteries of our faith "unlock" and explain one another. This type of comparison between Christian beliefs displays the coherence and unity of defined dogmas, which are the Church's infallible interpretations of Scripture.

Putting It All in Perspective   Perhaps the most important context of all we have saved for last: the interior life of the individual reader. What we get out of the Bible will largely depend on how we approach the Bible. Unless we are living a sustained and disciplined life of prayer, we will never have the reverence, the profound humility, or the grace we need to see the Scriptures for what they really are.

You are approaching the "word of God". But for thousands of years, since before he knit you in your mother's womb, the Word of God has been approaching you.

One Final Note. The volume you hold in your hands is only a small part of a much larger work still in production. Study helps similar to those printed in this booklet are being prepared for *all* the books of the Bible and will appear gradually as they are finished. Our ultimate goal is to publish a single, one-volume Study Bible that will include the entire text of Scripture, along with all the annotations, charts, cross-references, maps, and other features found in the following pages. Individual booklets will be published in the meantime, with the hope that God's people can begin to benefit from this labor before its full completion.

We have included a long list of Study Questions in the back to make this format as useful as possible, not only for individual study but for group settings and discussions as well. The questions are designed to help readers both "understand" the Bible and "apply" it to their lives. We pray that God will make use of our efforts and yours to help renew the face of the earth! «

INTRODUCTION TO THE GOSPEL ACCORDING TO MARK

Author The earliest manuscripts of the second Gospel are titled "According to Mark" (Gk. *Kata Markon*). This heading is not part of the original work but was added by the early Christians. It summarizes the Church's uniform tradition that Mark, a disciple of Simon Peter, wrote the second Gospel. Although Mark did not write as an eyewitness of Christ's public ministry, he was a channel of apostolic tradition through Peter, who was his primary source of information about the life of Jesus. His association with Peter is evident in both the NT and the testimony of the early Church. (1) Within the NT, Peter refers to his companionship with "my son Mark" in 1 Pet 5:13, and interpreters have noted that the general outline of Mark's Gospel is similar to Peter's presentation of the gospel in Acts 10:36–43. (2) Outside the NT, several Church Fathers insist that Peter's authority stands behind the second Gospel. Papias (A.D. 130) describes Mark as the "interpreter" of Peter, while Irenaeus (A.D. 180), Clement of Alexandria (A.D. 200), and Tertullian (A.D. 200) echo this tradition.

Few details exist about the life and character of Mark. He is known principally by his Roman name "Mark" (Lat. *Marcus*) but is sometimes called by his Jewish name "John" (Acts 12:25; 15:37). He is the cousin of the missionary Barnabas according to Col 4:10. More significantly, he was an associate of the Apostle Paul (Acts 12:25) and a welcome companion on Paul's first missionary journey (Acts 13:5). For reasons unstated, Mark withdrew prematurely from the mission (Acts 13:13), creating an awkward situation that later became a source of contention between him and Paul (Acts 15:36–41). At some point, however, Mark was reconciled with him and again became active in his ministry, since he is later present with Paul in Rome (Col 4:10; Philem 24) and, according to the apostle's estimation, "he [Mark] is very useful in serving me" (2 Tim 4:11). Tradition states that after the martyrdom of Peter and Paul, Mark was the first to establish churches in Alexandria in northern Egypt.

Date Two factors suggest that Mark completed his Gospel before A.D. 70, within one generation of the events he records. First, the Gospel itself points us in this direction. In Mk 13, Jesus prophesies the imminent destruction of Jerusalem and the Temple. This was fulfilled in A.D. 70, when the Romans violently destroyed the Holy City. Mark, however, makes no mention of this as a past event, nor does he give detailed information about the catastrophe that would indicate he was writing after the fact. Second, prominent traditions in the early Church date Mark's Gospel in the 60s A.D., or even earlier. Both a second-century document, called the Anti-Marcionite Prologue, and Irenaeus (A.D. 180) state that Mark wrote soon after Peter's martyrdom (c. A.D. 67)—a tradition that still allows for a date in the late 60s. Clement of Alexandria (A.D. 200), on the other hand, maintains that Mark wrote his Gospel *before* Peter's death. Still another witness, Eusebius (A.D. 340), fixes a date for Mark during the reign of the Emperor Claudius between A.D. 41 and 54. Although these varying traditions make it impossible for us to assign an exact date for the Gospel, they together suggest that Mark published his work sometime before A.D. 70.

Destination Mark wrote his Gospel primarily for Gentile believers in Imperial Rome. This is suggested by several considerations. (1) Mark regularly explains Jewish customs that would be unfamiliar to his readers (7:3–4; 14:12); (2) he translates Aramaic words and phrases (3:17; 5:41; 7:11, 34; 15:34); (3) he at times uses Latinized terms instead of their Greek equivalents (12:42; 15:16); (4) his story climaxes with a confession of faith by a Roman soldier (15:39). It is likely, moreover, that Mark's audience in Rome was at this time a target of fierce persecution under the depraved Emperor Nero (A.D. 64–68). His Gospel, then, is written to remind Roman believers of the suffering endured by their Lord and to encourage them to remain faithful during this time of trial.

Structure Mark's Gospel resists a neat and clearcut outline. As the narrator, Mark remains tucked behind his story and imposes no artificial structure on the traditions he has received; he is content, rather, to present the events of Jesus' life as he learned them. For the sake of convenience, however, the Gospel may be divided into two major sections and two minor sections (see outline). The two major sections (1:16—8:30; 8:31—15:47) comprise most of Mark's narrative and consist of various events that gradually build in momentum toward a climactic confession of faith. In the first movement (1:16—8:30), the story culminates with Peter's testimony, "You are the Christ" (8:29), a confession that stands out amid the surrounding confusion about Jesus' identity (8:28). Similarly, the second movement (8:31—15:47) ascends gradually and peaks with the centurion's declaration, "Truly this man was the Son of God!" (15:39), which also stands in contrast to the surrounding taunts leveled at Jesus (15:29–32, 36). The Gospel's two minor sections (1:1–15; 16:1–20) are small in size but great in importance. The Prologue (1:1–15) sets the stage for Jesus, narrating the preparations leading up to his public ministry. The Epilogue (16:1–20) crowns Mark's story with the account of Jesus' Resurrection and Ascension, bringing to a climax "the gospel of Jesus Christ" anticipated since the beginning (1:1).

Themes Mark paints a portrait of Jesus that is vivid and dynamic, focusing most of his attention on Jesus' mighty works. Apart from two lengthy sermons (4:1–32; 13:1–37), Mark depicts Jesus as an active healer and exorcist continually on the move—a feature the evangelist accentuates by using the word "immediately" over forty times in his mere sixteen chapters! In addition, Mark's Gospel engages the Christian reader with a number of rhetorical questions and statements that punctuate the story: "What is this? A new teaching!" (1:27); "Why does this man speak thus? . . . Who can forgive sins but God alone?" (2:7); "Who then is this, that even wind and sea obey him?" (4:41); "But who do you say that I am?" (8:29); "And what I say to you I say to all: Watch" (13:37). These statements address the attentive reader much as they address characters in the story. They invite every believer to look at Jesus with the eyes of faith, embrace him in hope, and imitate his heroic love.

The content of Mark's story revolves primarily around the identity of Jesus. Two aspects figure prominently: Jesus' secret and his divine Sonship. (1) *Secret.* In Mark, Jesus often attempts to conceal his identity as the Messiah because of the great possibility that his contemporaries will misunderstand his mission. During NT times, many in Israel expected the Messiah to liberate them from the oppressive rule of the Romans. For this reason they awaited an outstanding royal and military figure to subdue their enemies and reestablish the earthly kingdom of David in Jerusalem (11:10). Jesus distances himself from these popular, but mistaken, aspirations and instead works to conceal his messianic identity to avoid confusion about his ministry. When unclean spirits attempt to publicize his identity, Jesus silences them (1:25, 34; 3:12). When men try to announce Jesus as a miracle worker or Messiah, he orders them not to (5:43; 7:36; 8:26, 30; 9:9). Far from embracing the role of a political leader, Jesus labors to reconfigure messianic expectations through his example of servanthood and suffering. The true Messiah liberates God's people from the burdens of Satan, sickness, and sin—not the yoke of an earthly empire (1:27, 34, 41; 2:5, 17; 3:5, 10; 5:41; 7:37). (2) *Sonship.* The divine Sonship of Jesus is also a leading theme in Mark. It could be said, in fact, that recognizing Jesus as the divine Son of God is the goal of Mark's Gospel. Ironically, Jesus' Sonship and Incarnation are mysteries hidden from most of the Gospel's characters, despite repeated suggestions and hints pointing in this direction. As the narrator, Mark introduces Jesus from the outset as "the Son of God" (1:1). The demons are aware of it (3:11; 5:7), God the Father twice proclaims it in public (1:11; 9:7), and Jesus himself affirms it in no uncertain terms (14:61–62). Only at the Crucifixion is the Sonship of Jesus fully recognized as he surrenders his life with love to the Father. It is here that a single Gospel character (Roman centurion) confesses Jesus as "the Son of God" (15:39). Mark's Gospel proclaims this mystery of Christ's Sonship in story form and seeks both to inform and to challenge readers with this central truth of the gospel.

OUTLINE OF THE GOSPEL ACCORDING TO MARK

1. Prologue: Preparations for the Messiah and His Forerunner (1:1–15)
   A. Preaching and Ministry of John the Baptist (1:1–8)
   B. Baptism of Jesus by John (1:9–11)
   C. Testing of Jesus by Satan (1:12–13)
   D. Jesus Begins to Preach the Gospel (1:14–15)

2. Public Ministry: The Messiah's Secret and His Widespread Ministry (1:16—8:30)
   A. Jesus Becomes Popular and Controversial in Galilee (1:16—3:12)
   B. Jesus Teaches the Apostles through Words and Deeds (3:13—7:23)
   C. Jesus Travels to Gentile Regions (7:24—8:30)

3. Passion Narrative: The Suffering Messiah and Passion Week Narratives (8:31—15:47)
   A. Passion Predictions and Formation of Disciples on the Way to Jerusalem (8:31—10:52)
   B. Jesus' Entry into Jerusalem and His Conflict in the Temple (11:1—13:37)
   C. Last Supper, Trials, and Crucifixion of Jesus (14:1—15:47)

4. Resurrection Epilogue: The Risen Messiah and Easter Narratives(16:1–20)
   A. Empty Tomb of Jesus (16:1–8)
   B. Resurrection Appearances and Great Commission (16:9–18)
   C. Jesus' Ascension and the Spread of the Gospel (16:19–20)

THE GOSPEL ACCORDING TO
MARK

The Preaching of John the Baptist

The beginning of the gospel of Jesus Christ, the Son of God.[a]

2 As it is written in Isaiah the prophet,[b]

"Behold, I send my messenger before your face,
who shall prepare your way;

3 the voice of one crying in the wilderness:
Prepare the way of the Lord,
make his paths straight—"

[4]John the baptizer appeared[c] in the wilderness, preaching a baptism of repentance for the forgiveness of sins. [5]And there went out to him all the country of Judea, and all the people of Jerusalem; and they were baptized by him in the river Jordan, confessing their sins. [6]Now John was clothed with camel's hair, and had a leather belt around his waist, and ate locusts and wild honey. [7]And he preached, saying, "After me comes he who is mightier than I, the thong of whose sandals I am not worthy to stoop down and untie. [8]I have baptized you with water; but he will baptize you with the Holy Spirit."

The Baptism of Jesus

9 In those days Jesus came from Nazareth of Galilee and was baptized by John in the Jordan. [10]And when he came up out of the water, immediately he saw the heavens opened and the Spirit

---

1:2–8: Mt 3:1–12; Lk 3:2–16; Jn 1:6, 15, 19–28. **1:2:** Mal 3:1; Mt 11:10; Lk 7:27. **1:3:** Is 40:3.
1:4: Acts 13:24. **1:9–11:** Mt 3:13–17; Lk 3:21–22; Jn 1:29–34.

1:1 The beginning: The opening verse is a title for the entire Gospel. **the gospel:** The "good news" that Christ has come to *rescue* all nations from sin, selfishness, and Satan and to *reveal* the inner life of God to the world. This is accomplished as Jesus inaugurates the kingdom of God (1:15). **the Son of God:** The predominant title for Jesus in Mark (1:1; 3:11; 5:7; 9:7; 12:6; 14:61; 15:39; CCC 422, 515). Both the works (miracles) and words (teaching) of Jesus substantiate this claim to divine Sonship, while the Father announces it publicly at his Baptism (1:11) and Transfiguration (9:7).

1:2–3 Mark outlines the mission of John and Jesus by splicing together three OT passages: Is 40:3, Ex 23:20, and Mal 3:1. • The Exodus passage recalls how Yahweh appointed a messenger (angel) to lead Israel from the slavery of Egypt to the safety of the Promised Land. Isaiah projects this memory from the distant past into the future, announcing that both Israel and the nations will experience a New Exodus in the messianic age. Preparations are in order for a new Deliverer, the Suffering Servant, who will bring the nations from the darkness of sin and idolatry to the light of Mt. Zion. Malachi's oracle presents the dark side of this scenario, warning Jerusalem that the coming of the messianic Lord will mean disaster if the shepherds of Israel are unprepared to welcome his arrival. For Mark, these passages are linked together by a common call to prepare the "way" of the Lord: John is the herald who points out the "way" of this New Exodus, while Jesus is the "Lord" and Suffering Servant who accomplishes it. This is the only time Mark quotes directly from the OT as the Gospel narrator. See note on 8:27–10:52.

1:5 baptized by him: The baptism of John signified the need for inner purity but did not effect this in a sacramental way. John was fully aware that his disciples must also receive the greater Baptism of the Messiah, which both signifies and effects spiritual cleansing. Only the Christian sacrament washes the soul of sin, infuses the grace of divine sonship, and regenerates the believer in the Holy Spirit (Jn 3:5; Acts 2:38;

Tit 3:5; CCC 718–20). **in the river Jordan:** The main river in Palestine and a suitable location to baptize large numbers. • The Jordan is linked with stories of deliverance in the OT. Here the Israelites crossed over to inherit the Promised Land (Josh 3:14–17). Here too Naaman the Syrian (a Gentile) was cleansed of leprosy (2 Kings 5:14). Against this twofold background John's ministry at the Jordan prepares for the salvation of Israel and the Gentiles by the Messiah.

1:6 John was clothed: Garments of animal skin were the distinctive attire of OT prophets (Zech 13:4). • John's appearance recalls that of Elijah (2 Kings 1:8), and his presence at the Jordan recalls the site where Elijah departed into heaven (2 Kings 2:6–11). See note on 9:11. **ate locusts:** One of a few clean (kosher) insects that God permitted the Israelites to eat under the Old Covenant (Lev 11:22). This detail portrays John as faithful to the Torah and highlights his renunciation of worldly comforts. His disciplined life-style also included fasting (2:18).

1:7 I am not worthy: Evidence of John's humility. Removing and carrying **sandals** was a menial task reserved for slaves serving their master. John regards himself as unworthy to perform even a slave's task for the Messiah. • *Allegorically* (St. Gregory the Great, *Hom. in Evan.* 7), Jesus' sandals, made from the skins of dead animals, represent mankind dead in sin. Once Christ clothed himself with our nature in the Incarnation, the miracle proved so profound that not even John was able to unfasten or explain this mystery of God-made-man.

1:9–11 The Baptism of Jesus. As One who is sinless, Jesus has no actual need for repentance (Heb 4:15; 1 Pet 2:22). He nevertheless receives John's baptism to identify with sinners as part of the Father's plan to save them (CCC 536). The **voice** of the Father, the Baptism of the **Son**, and the descent of the **Spirit** mark this episode as a revelation of the Blessed Trinity. See note on Mt 3:15.

1:10 the heavens opened: The underlying expression is more dramatic than the translation, since the Greek verb *schizō* means to "rip" or "tear". Heaven was thus "torn open" at the sound of God's voice and the descent of the Spirit (Is 64:1). Elsewhere in Mark this same verb depicts the tearing of the Temple veil (15:38), an episode similarly accompanied by a

---

[a] Other ancient authorities omit *the Son of God.*
[b] Other ancient authorities read *in the prophets.*
[c] Other ancient authorities read *John was baptizing.*

descending upon him like a dove; [11]and a voice came from heaven, "You are my beloved Son;[d] with you I am well pleased."

The Temptation of Jesus

12 The Spirit immediately drove him out into the wilderness. [13]And he was in the wilderness forty days, tempted by Satan; and he was with the wild beasts; and the angels ministered to him.

Jesus Preaches the Gospel in Galilee

14 Now after John was arrested, Jesus came into Galilee, preaching the gospel of God, [15]and saying, "The time is fulfilled, and the kingdom of God is at hand; repent, and believe in the gospel."

Jesus Calls the First Disciples

16 And passing along by the Sea of Galilee, he saw Simon and Andrew the brother of Simon cast-

ing a net in the sea; for they were fishermen. [17]And Jesus said to them, "Follow me and I will make you become fishers of men." [18]And immediately they left their nets and followed him. [19]And going on a little farther, he saw James the son of Zeb'edee and John his brother, who were in their boat mending the nets. [20]And immediately he called them; and they left their father Zeb'edee in the boat with the hired servants, and followed him.

The Man with an Unclean Spirit

21 And they went into Caper'na-um; and immediately on the sabbath he entered the synagogue and taught. [22]And they were astonished at his teaching, for he taught them as one who had authority, and not as the scribes. [23]And immediately

---

1:11: Ps 2:7; Is 42:1.   **1:12–13:** Mt 4:1–11; Lk 4:1–13.   **1:14–15:** Mt 4:12–17; Lk 4:14–15.
1:16–20: Mt 4:18–22; Lk 5:1–11; Jn 1:40–42.   **1:21–22:** Mt 7:28–29; Lk 4:31–32.

---

declaration of Jesus' Sonship (15:39). **a dove:** An image with various associations in the Bible (Song 1:15; 6:9; Hos 11:11; Mt 10:16). • A close connection between the Spirit and a dove is found in Genesis: as the "Spirit of God" hovered over the waters at creation (Gen 1:2), so Noah sent forth a "dove" to hover over the flood waters once creation was cleansed and renewed (Gen 8:10–12). Jesus' Baptism likewise inaugurates a new beginning for the world through the Spirit and prefigures our own cleansing through Baptism (1 Pet 3:18–22; CCC 536, 694, 701). See note on Mt 3:11.

1:11 my beloved Son: The Father's announcement echoes several OT passages. • (1) Isaiah 42:1 prophecies the coming of God's pleasing Servant, who will rescue Israel (Is 42:7) and be a "light to the nations" (Is 42:6). Jesus fulfills this role as the Suffering Servant (10:45) and light of the world (Jn 8:12). (2) Psalm 2:7 portrays King David as the anointed son of God. Jesus is here the royal Son anointed by the Spirit (Lk 4:18; Rom 1:3). (3) The same title was once given to Isaac, where the Greek OT translates "only son" in Gen 22:2, 12, as "my beloved son". As Abraham's near-sacrifice of Isaac procured a

---

[d] Or *my Son, my* (or *the*) *Beloved.*

WORD STUDY

Repentance (1:4)

Metanoia (Gk.): literally a "change of mind". The word is used 22 times in the NT for a conversion of one's entire life to the Lord. Based on similar OT concepts, it involves a twofold movement of the heart: one who repents turns *away* from sin (1 Kings 8:35; Ezek 18:30) and *toward* God (Hos 6:1; Sir 17:25, 26; Heb 6:1). This entails genuine contrition for past failings and a firm resolve to avoid them in the future, and it may be accompanied by bodily disciplines like fasting (Dan 9:3–5; Joel 2:12; 2 Cor 7:10). Because repentance is a gradual process of transformation, God is patient with sinners struggling to make amends and redirect their lives toward holiness (Wis 12:10; Rom 2:4; 2 Pet 3:9). Repentance is inspired by the eternal life offered in Christ (Mk 1:15; Acts 2:38), and its genuineness becomes evident when lives are changed in accord with the gospel (Mt 3:8; Acts 26:20; Gal 5:22–24).

divine oath of worldwide blessing (Gen 22:16–18), so Jesus is sent by the Father to fulfill this covenant oath and unleash the blessings promised to the patriarch (Jn 3:16; Rom 8:32).

1:12–13 An abridged account of Jesus' temptation. • Jesus faces the same ordeal that Adam and Israel endured in the OT (CCC 538–540). He is thus **tempted by Satan** among the **wild beasts,** as the first Adam was tempted amid the beasts in paradise. He likewise retraces the steps of Israel, being led into the **wilderness** by the **Spirit** and tested for **forty days** as the Israelites marched in the desert for 40 years of testing. In the end, Jesus succeeds where Adam and Israel failed by resisting the devil and proving his filial love for the Father. This initiates an extended campaign against demons, death, and disease throughout the Gospel (1:25, 31, 34; 2:11; 3:5; 5:13, 39–41). See note on Mt 4:1–11. • Morally (St. John Chrysostom, *Hom. in Matt.* 13), Jesus endured temptation to train his disciples how to overcome the devil. No one should be surprised, then, that after our own Baptism the tempter assails us more aggressively than before. Victory is assured if, like Jesus, we commit ourselves to fasting, wait upon the Lord with patience, and have no desire for things beyond our need.

1:14 John was arrested: A pivotal event turning the focus of Jesus' ministry to Galilee. Prior to this, Jesus had an earlier ministry in Judea that overlapped with John's (Jn 3:23). See note on Mt 4:12.

1:15 the kingdom of God: God's sovereign rule over all nations through Jesus. • The kingdom of Christ is closely linked with the ancient kingdom of Israel that flourished under David and Solomon. Although David's empire soon collapsed, for a brief time it foreshadowed the glory of Christ's reign over the tribes of Israel (2 Sam 5:1–5; Mt 19:28) and other Gentile nations (1 Kings 4:20–21; Mt 28:18–20). The international kingdom of old is now resurrected and transfigured in the Church, where Christ rules as David's rightful heir (Mt 1:1; Lk 1:32–33) enthroned in heaven (Mk 16:19; Heb 8:1–2).

1:16–20 The first disciples respond to Jesus **immediately** (1:18, 20). His compelling invitation to **follow** as a disciple is Jesus' initial step toward sending missionaries into the world as **fishers of men** (Mt 28:18–20). Christ chooses men of modest education to demonstrate to the world that the wisdom of the gospel stems directly from God and not the ingenuity of man. See chart: *The Twelve Apostles* at Mk 3.

1:20 left their father: Such an abrupt break with family and livelihood was extraordinary then as now. The impulse to abandon everything and follow Jesus highlights the surpassing excellence of Christian discipleship over every worldly pursuit. **hired servants:** Suggests that the fishing enterprise of Zebedee and his sons was prosperous.

1:21 Capernaum: Jesus' new home and headquarters in

there was in their synagogue a man with an unclean spirit; ²⁴and he cried out, "What have you to do with us, Jesus of Nazareth? Have you come to destroy us? I know who you are, the Holy One of God." ²⁵But Jesus rebuked him, saying, "Be silent, and come out of him!" ²⁶And the unclean spirit, convulsing him and crying with a loud voice, came out of him. ²⁷And they were all amazed, so that they questioned among themselves, saying, "What is this? A new teaching! With authority he commands even the unclean spirits, and they obey him." ²⁸And at once his fame spread everywhere throughout all the surrounding region of Galilee.

Healings at Simon's House

29 And immediately he ᵉ left the synagogue, and entered the house of Simon and Andrew, with James and John. ³⁰Now Simon's mother-in-law lay sick with a fever, and immediately they told him of her. ³¹And he came and took her by the hand and lifted her up, and the fever left her; and she served them.

32 That evening, at sundown, they brought to him all who were sick or possessed with demons. ³³And the whole city was gathered together about the door. ³⁴And he healed many who were sick with various diseases, and cast out many demons; and he would not permit the demons to speak, because they knew him.

Jesus Preaches and Heals throughout Galilee

35 And in the morning, a great while before day, he rose and went out to a lonely place, and there he prayed. ³⁶And Simon and those who were with him followed him, ³⁷and they found him and said to him, "Every one is searching for you." ³⁸And he said to them, "Let us go on to the next towns, that I may preach there also; for that is why I came out." ³⁹And he went throughout all Galilee, preaching in their synagogues and casting out demons.

Jesus Cleanses a Leper

40 And a leper came to him begging him, and kneeling said to him, "If you will, you can make me clean." ⁴¹Moved with pity, he stretched out his hand and touched him, and said to him, "I will; be clean." ⁴²And immediately the leprosy left him, and he was made clean. ⁴³And he sternly charged him, and sent him away at once, ⁴⁴and said to him, "See that you say nothing to any one; but go, show yourself to the priest, and offer for your cleansing what Moses commanded, for a proof to the people." ᶠ ⁴⁵But he went out and began to talk freely about it, and to spread the news, so that Jesus ᵍ could no longer openly enter a town, but was out in the country; and people came to him from every quarter.

Jesus Heals a Paralytic

2 And when he returned to Caper′na-um after some days, it was reported that he was at home. ²And many were gathered together, so that there was no longer room for them, not even about the door; and he was preaching the word to them. ³And they came, bringing to him a paralytic carried by four men. ⁴And when they could not get near him

1:23–28: Lk 4:33–37. **1:24:** Jn 6:69. **1:29–31:** Mt 8:14–15; Lk 4:38–39. **1:32–34:** Mt 8:16–17; Lk 4:40–41.
1:35–38: Lk 4:42–43. **1:39:** Mt 4:23–25; Lk 4:44. **1:40–45:** Mt 8:2–4; Lk 5:12–16. **1:44:** Lev 13:49; 14:2–32.
2:3–12: Mt 9:2–8; Lk 5:18–26.

Galilee (2:1; Mt 4:12–13). It is located on the northern shore of the Sea of Galilee. **on the sabbath:** The seventh day of the Jewish week set aside for worship and rest (Gen 2:3; Ex 20:8–11; CCC 2168–73). Since Jews number the days from sunset to sunset, the Sabbath begins every Friday evening and ends at sundown Saturday. **synagogue:** A small building used as a gathering place for prayer, worship, and instruction in the Scriptures. See note on Mt 4:23.

1:23 an unclean spirit: A demon or fallen angel (3:11; 5:2; 6:7; 9:25). He confesses that Jesus is the "Holy One" (1:24) out of fear, not genuine faith (cf. Jas 2:19).

1:27 With authority: Divine power is displayed through Jesus' word. While most exorcists of the day recited lengthy incantations or used odorous roots to expel demons, Jesus simply commands the spirits and they leave (CCC 550). The demons' inability to resist him is shown by their dramatic exhibition of "convulsing" and "crying" (1:26).

1:32 That evening: i.e., after sunset on the Sabbath (Saturday). Bringing the sick and demon-possessed to Jesus was laborious and thus unlawful before the Sabbath day ended. See note on 1:21.

1:35 in the morning: Following Mark's chronology, Jesus prayed early Sunday morning following the Sabbath. His practice anticipates the liturgical prayer of the Church early on the first day of the week (CCC 2174). Jesus also practices what he preaches on the propriety of solitary prayer (Mt 6:5–6; CCC 2602). See note on 1:32.

1:40 a leper: Leprosy was a skin disease that made victims unclean, i.e., unfit to participate in the liturgical life of Israel (Lev 13:1–8). Because ritual uncleanness was considered contagious under the Old Covenant—infecting everyone who came in contact with it—lepers were isolated from society to keep those who were clean separated from those who were unclean (Lev 13:45–46). Jesus reaches across this divide when he touches the leper, and though others would be defiled by such contact, he conquers the uncleanness by the greater power of his holiness (1:41; CCC 1503–5). See note on Mt 8:1–9:38.

1:44 say nothing to any one: The "messianic secret" is a leading theme in Mark. Jesus frequently enjoins silence on demons (1:25, 34; 3:12) and men (5:43; 7:36; 8:30; 9:9) to conceal his identity as the Messiah (CCC 439). Several considerations account for this strategy. (1) Jesus wanted to avoid a sensationalist reputation of being no more than a wonder-worker. Publicizing his deeds by word of mouth comes with the danger that rumors will begin to disconnect his miracles from his saving message. (2) He wanted to sidestep popular expectations that the Messiah would be a political and military leader. (3) He did not wish to ignite the wrath of his enemies before the appointed time of his Passion. See introduction: *Themes.* **show yourself:** The Mosaic Law required Levitical priests to inspect lepers and determine their status as clean or unclean (Lev 14:1–32). With approval, an individual pronounced clean would offer sacrifices at the Temple to be reinstated in the community of Israel. See note on Mt 8:4.

2:1–12 The healing of the paralytic reveals Jesus' identity through his actions: he claims to forgive sins as only God can forgive and to channel that forgiveness to the world as only the

ᵉ Other ancient authorities read *they.*
ᶠ Greek *to them.*
ᵍ Greek *he.*

because of the crowd, they removed the roof above him; and when they had made an opening, they let down the pallet on which the paralytic lay. ⁵And when Jesus saw their faith, he said to the paralytic, "My son, your sins are forgiven." ⁶Now some of the scribes were sitting there, questioning in their hearts, ⁷"Why does this man speak like this? It is blasphemy! Who can forgive sins but God alone?" ⁸And immediately Jesus, perceiving in his spirit that they questioned like this within themselves, said to them, "Why do you question like this in your hearts? ⁹Which is easier, to say to the paralytic, 'Your sins are forgiven,' or to say, 'Rise, take up your pallet and walk'? ¹⁰But that you may know that the Son of man has authority on earth to forgive sins"—he said to the paralytic—¹¹"I say to you, rise, take up your pallet and go home." ¹²And he rose, and immediately took up the pallet and went out before them all; so that they were all amazed and glorified God, saying, "We never saw anything like this!"

Jesus Calls Levi

13 He went out again beside the sea; and all the crowd gathered about him, and he taught them. ¹⁴And as he passed on, he saw Levi the son of Alphae´us sitting at the tax office, and he said to him, "Follow me." And he rose and followed him.

15 And as he sat at table in his house, many tax collectors and sinners were sitting with Jesus and his disciples; for there were many who followed him. ¹⁶And the scribes of ^{h} the Pharisees, when they saw that he was eating with sinners and tax collectors, said to his disciples, "Why does he eat ^{i} with tax collectors and sinners?" ¹⁷And when Jesus heard it, he said to them, "Those who are well have no need of a physician, but those who are sick; I came not to call the righteous, but sinners."

The Question about Fasting

18 Now John's disciples and the Pharisees were fasting; and people came and said to him, "Why do John's disciples and the disciples of the Pharisees fast, but your disciples do not fast?" ¹⁹And Jesus

---

2:12: Mt 9:33.   **2:14–17:** Mt 9:9–13; Lk 5:27–32.   **2:16:** Acts 23:9.
2:18–22: Mt 9:14–17; Lk 5:33–38.

Jerusalem Temple and priesthood were authorized to do under the Old Covenant.

2:5 their faith: i.e., the faith of the four men who carried the paralytic (2:4). ● The forgiveness that Jesus confers upon the helpless paralytic in response to the faith of others (the four men) mirrors the effects of Infant Baptism, where he continues to regenerate helpless children through the intercessory faith of their parents (CCC 1250–53).

2:6 the scribes: Scholars of the Mosaic Law and its traditional interpretation. With the exception of one episode (12:28–34), they are cast as Jesus' adversaries in Mark.

2:7 It is blasphemy!: The scribes are incensed that Jesus claims for himself a prerogative that belongs only to God: the power to remit sins (Ps 103:3; Is 43:25; CCC 1441). They have misjudged the matter as blasphemy, which was a capital crime in ancient Israel (Lev 24:16). Note that Jesus manifests his divinity both by absolving the man's sins and by exposing the unspoken disapproval of his critics (2:8).

2:9 Which is easier: Forgiveness is easier to claim than to accomplish, since its effects cannot be verified by observation. For this reason, Jesus restores the man's body as a visible demonstration of what he has already done invisibly in his soul. See note on Mt 9:8.

2:14 Levi: Also called "Matthew" (Mt 9:9). He abandoned his occupation to follow Jesus and was later named an apostle (3:18). **the tax office:** The Pharisees despised tax collectors as "sinners" (2:15) for several reasons. (1) Collecting revenue in Galilee involved frequent contact with Gentiles. By Pharisaic standards, this meant that collectors were exposed to the ritual defilement of the pagans. (2) Since taxes were collected for the unwelcome Romans, who ruled Palestine, collectors were branded as traitors to Israel's hope for national independence. (3) Collectors were sometimes guilty of extortion, exacting personal commissions above the required tax amount.

2:15–28 Three controversies between Jesus and the Pharisees. In each, the Pharisees try to discredit Jesus as a spiritual leader (2:16, 18, 24). They consider his behavior questionable and even dangerous, as though Jesus were leading Israel away from true covenant holiness. (1) In 2:15–17, the Pharisees are scandalized by those *with whom* Jesus eats (tax collectors, sin-

ners). (2) In 2:18–22, they question *why* he eats with his disciples instead of fasting like John's followers. (3) In 2:23–28, the issue concerns *when* his disciples pluck and eat grain (on the Sabbath). These tensions reach the breaking point with the Pharisees' conspiracy to eliminate Jesus (3:6).

2:16 eating with sinners: Table-fellowship was symbolic of personal acceptance and mutual friendship in the ancient Near East. Jesus' open association with outcasts thus violates the standards of the **Pharisees**, who regarded sinners and tax collectors as inappropriate company for the religious Jew. They clung to Old Covenant standards of holiness that required Israelites to separate themselves from all sources of uncleanness, including fellowship with Gentiles (Acts 10:28). Jesus exemplifies New Covenant holiness, which extends mercy to everyone in imitation of the Father (Mt 5:43–48; Lk 6:36; CCC 545, 574). See essay: *Who Are the Pharisees?*

2:17 no need of a physician: A well-known proverb. Jesus adapts it to imply that table-fellowship is central to his healing mission. Just as doctors do not avoid the sick, so Jesus cannot avoid those wounded by sin. **not to call the righteous:** Jesus did not come to prolong the Old Covenant with the nation of Israel. This was an imperfect, provisional covenant designed to separate Israel from the Gentiles and their sins (Lev 20:26) while Israel was not ready to love God from the heart (Jer 11:8; Mt 19:8). Jesus inaugurates the New Covenant to transform the hearts of his people (Jer 31:31–34; Mt 5:8) and so welcomes all into God's covenant family. Whereas the Old Covenant quarantined Israel from the world, the New Covenant embraces the world within God's mercy (Rom 11:32).

2:19 the bridegroom: Jesus uses marital imagery to reveal his divinity. ● His words recall several OT passages that depict Yahweh as a groom wedded to Israel (Is 54:5; Jer 3:20; Hos 2:20). The NT transfers this covenant relationship to Christ as the divine spouse of the Church (Mt 25:1–13; Eph 5:25; CCC 796). **they cannot fast:** Since fasting symbolizes mourning and separation, it was inappropriate while Jesus was present among the disciples. ● Christians fast before celebrating the liturgy, i.e., before Christ comes among them in Word and Sacrament. The arrival of Christ then makes it a time of feasting, when the divine Bridegroom gives himself in love to his bride, the Church. Communion with Jesus in the Eucharist is a foretaste of the heavenly "marriage supper of the Lamb" (Rev 19:9).

---

^{h} Other ancient authorities read *and.*
^{i} Other ancient authorities add *and drink.*

Who Are the Pharisees?

THE Pharisees are part of a Jewish renewal movement that appears frequently in the NT. In almost every instance, they stand beneath dark clouds of suspicion and controversy. The Gospels depict them as the critical opponents of Jesus, his teaching, and his mission. The Pharisees seem to lurk behind every corner, waiting to trap Jesus and discredit him before the crowds. What is the source of this conflict? Why were the Pharisees so threatened by Jesus and his proclamation of God's kingdom?

From biblical and extrabiblical information it is evident that the Pharisees advocated a religious program quite at odds with the gospel of the New Covenant. Although not Israel's official teachers or leaders, the Pharisees were popular and held great sway with the masses. They were deeply concerned with the cultural and religious crisis of the day: How does one live as a faithful Jew in a land that is ruled and occupied by pagans (Romans)? The Pharisees' answer: Israel must separate itself from all Gentile impurity and defilement, since only in this way will God rescue his people from the clutches of Rome. Even their name—which means the "separated ones" (Heb. *perushim*)—underscores this national agenda.

At a practical level, the Pharisees' quest for holiness and separation was expressed in a number of ways.

(1) The Pharisees gave considerable attention to ritual purity.

They looked to the Temple and priests of Jerusalem, considering the elaborate purity requirements for priests (Lev 21-22) a fitting model for Jewish purity in the homes of laypeople. All Israelites, the Pharisees reasoned, should maintain this high level of priestlike holiness in their personal lives. Related to this:

(2) The Pharisees tightened their grip on Israel's national symbols.

Circumcision (Lev 12:3), the Sabbath day (Ex 20:8-11), food laws (Lev 11), and tithing (Deut 14:22-29) were all expressions of Israel's unique covenant with God upon which the Pharisees laid great stress. Scrupulous observance of these laws meant that the Pharisees could proudly assert their identity in the midst of their Gentile neighbors. In addition to God's written law (Gen-Deut):

(3) The Pharisees developed an entire body of personal rituals and traditions to stand alongside the books of Moses.

These embodied Pharisaic interpretations of the Law and functioned as supplements to the Law. They included practices like cleansing hands and utensils before preparing or eating food (Mk 7:3-4).

This background sets the clashes between Jesus and the Pharisees in a whole new light. The Pharisees attached themselves to the destiny of Old Covenant Israel, while Jesus was inaugurating the international New Covenant in the Church. The Pharisees tried to insulate Israel from the Gentiles, while Jesus was reaching out to embrace the nations with God's mercy. The Pharisees were religious separatists, while Jesus' proclamation of God's kingdom was open and inclusive.

For these reasons, Jesus offers a harsh critique of the Pharisees (Mt 23). Their tenacious concern for ritual exactness and outward observances distracted them from the most important matters of God's Law: "justice and mercy and faith" (Mt 23:23). The Pharisees' inordinate concern with Jewish nationalism became the idol that blocked their way into the kingdom.

In the Gospels, this smoldering tension ignited as Jesus challenged their views on the Sabbath (Mt 12:1-14), ritual purity (Mk 7:1-23), table-fellowship (Mt 9:10-13), tithing (Mt 23:23), and divorce (Mt 19:1-9). He charged many of them with hypocrisy (Lk 12:1) and a misplaced confidence in Pharisaic piety (Lk 18:9-14).

In the end, Jesus' conflicts with the Pharisees had little to do with isolated disagreements over the Torah and everything to do with God's saving plan for Israel and the world.

The arrival of Christ's New Covenant signaled the end of Israel's separation from Gentiles and the beginning of a worldwide family of God. «

said to them, "Can the wedding guests fast while the bridegroom is with them? As long as they have the bridegroom with them, they cannot fast. [20]The days will come, when the bridegroom is taken away from them, and then they will fast in that day. [21]No one sews a piece of unshrunk cloth on an old garment; if he does, the patch tears away from it, the new from the old, and a worse tear is made. [22]And no one puts new wine into old wineskins; if he does, the wine will burst the skins, and the wine is lost, and so are the skins; but new wine is for fresh skins."[j]

A Teaching about the Sabbath

23 One sabbath he was going through the grainfields; and as they made their way his disciples began to pluck heads of grain. [24]And the Pharisees said to him, "Look, why are they doing what is not lawful on the sabbath?" [25]And he said to them, "Have you never read what David did, when he was in need and was hungry, he and those who were with him: [26]how he entered the house of God, when Abi´athar was high priest, and ate the bread of the Presence, which it is not lawful for any but the priests to eat, and also gave it to those who were with him?" [27]And he said to them, "The sabbath was made for man, not man for the sabbath; [28]so the Son of man is lord even of the sabbath."

The Man with a Withered Hand

3 Again he entered the synagogue, and a man was there who had a withered hand. [2]And they watched him, to see whether he would heal him on the sabbath, so that they might accuse him. [3]And he said to the man who had the withered hand, "Come here." [4]And he said to them, "Is it lawful on the sabbath to do good or to do harm, to save life or to kill?" But they were silent. [5]And he looked around at them with anger, grieved at their hardness of heart, and said to the man, "Stretch out your hand." He stretched it out, and his hand was restored. [6]The Pharisees went out, and immediately held counsel with the Hero´dians against him, how to destroy him.

A Multitude by the Sea

7 Jesus withdrew with his disciples to the sea, and a great multitude from Galilee followed; also from Judea [8]and Jerusalem and Idume´a and from beyond the Jordan and from about Tyre and Sidon a great multitude, hearing all that he did, came to him. [9]And he told his disciples to have a boat ready for him because of the crowd, lest they should crush him; [10]for he had healed many, so that all who

---

2:20: Lk 17:22.　**2:23–28:** Mt 12:1–8; Lk 6:1–5.　**2:23:** Deut 23:25.　**2:26:** 1 Sam 21:1–6; 2 Sam 8:17.
2:27: Ex 23:12; Deut 5:14.　**3:1–6:** Mt 12:9–14; Lk 6:6–11.　**3:2:** Lk 11:54.　**3:6:** Mk 12:13.
3:7–12: Mt 4:24–25; 12:15–16; Lk 6:17–19.　**3:8:** Mt 11:21.

2:21–22 Because the Old Covenant has become like an **old garment** and **old wineskins**, the New Covenant can neither be stitched to its worn fibers nor poured into its brittle skins. Rather, the *fasting* and anticipation of the Old Covenant must give way to the *feasting* and celebration of the New Covenant that Jesus brings into the world.
2:24 not lawful on the sabbath: Although Deut 23:25 permits the Israelites to pluck and eat standing grain, the Pharisees indict the disciples under the law of Ex 34:21, which forbids harvesting on the Sabbath (Ex 20:8–11; CCC 2168–73). Resolved to discredit him, the Pharisees equate plucking grain with harvesting it.
2:25 Have you never read: A stinging insult to the educated Pharisees. See note on Mt 12:3. **what David did:** Jesus recalls 1 Sam 21:1–6 to shed light on the present circumstances. ● David was permitted to override the Mosaic ritual Law by letting his hungry companions eat the sacred bread of the Tabernacle reserved for the priests. Since Jesus is the Messiah and thus greater than David (12:35–37), he should not be condemned for suspending the Sabbath to meet a legitimate need (hunger) for his own disciples. Should the Pharisees denounce Jesus, they would unwittingly denounce the honored King David.
2:26 when Abiathar was high priest: The priest who provided David with bread was actually Ahimelech, Abiathar's father (1 Sam 21:1). This apparent discrepancy causes some modern scholars to accuse Jesus of misquoting Scripture, although this conclusion is unnecessary. ● Jesus probably mentioned Abiathar instead of Ahimelech to post a warning for the Pharisees. Abiathar is infamous in OT history as the last high priest of his line, who was banished from Jerusalem and the priesthood for opposing Solomon, the son of David and the heir of his kingdom (1 Kings 2:26–27). He thus represents the end of an old order that passes away with the coming

of David's royal successor. As Jesus compares himself and the disciples with David and his men, he likewise draws the Pharisees into the story by casting them as figures like Abiathar. The Pharisees, then, represent an old order of covenant leadership that is about to expire, and if they persist in their opposition to Jesus, the new heir of the Davidic kingdom, they will meet the same disastrous fate that befell Abiathar. Jesus' allusion to this OT tradition was a subtle yet strategic way to caution the Pharisees against their antagonism to his ministry.
2:27 the sabbath: A day for physical rest and spiritual worship (Gen 2:1–3; Ex 20:8–11). It reminded the Israelites weekly of their total dependence upon God. The Pharisees, however, made observance of the Sabbath according to their own standards a stringent test of Jewish faithfulness. Whoever disobeyed the minute Sabbath regulations codified by the Pharisees was automatically suspected of religious laxity or compromise. According to Jesus, God designed the Sabbath to benefit his people, not to burden them (CCC 2172–73).
3:4 Is it lawful . . . ?: Jesus implies that doing **good** for the sake of mercy or necessity does not constitute a violation of the Sabbath. One should abstain from servile works, not good works. **or to kill?:** An alarming alternative to saving life. Common sympathy might allow for the preservation of life on the Sabbath, but not its destruction. ● Jesus may allude to the precedent of 1 Macc 2:41, where the Jews temporarily suspended Sabbath observance to permit defensive warfare. This was necessary in order to **save life** from military attacks on their sacred day of rest. If Israel could sidestep the Sabbath to preserve life, then surely Jesus can heal a man's hand on the same day. See note on Lk 6:9.
3:6 Pharisees . . . Herodians: Two religious and political groups in NT Palestine. They held opposite political stances and outlooks on Jewish life but stood united in their opposition to Jesus (CCC 574). See note on 12:13.
3:7–12 Jesus gains widespread popularity with the crowds. Although they perceive him as a powerful healer and exorcist,

---

[j] Other ancient authorities omit *but new wine is for fresh skins*.

had diseases pressed upon him to touch him. [11]And whenever the unclean spirits saw him, they fell down before him and cried out, "You are the Son of God." [12]And he strictly ordered them not to make him known.

Jesus Appoints the Twelve

13 And he went up into the hills, and called to him those whom he desired; and they came to him. [14]And he appointed twelve,[k] to be with him, and to be sent out to preach [15]and have authority to cast out demons: [16]Simon whom he surnamed Peter; [17]James the son of Zeb′edee and John the brother of James, whom he surnamed Bo-aner′ges, that is, sons of thunder; [18]Andrew, and Philip, and Bartholomew, and Matthew, and Thomas, and James the son of Alphae′us, and Thaddaeus, and Simon the Cananaean, [19]and Judas Iscariot, who betrayed him.

Jesus and Beelzebul

Then he went home; [20]and the crowd came together again, so that they could not even eat. [21]And when his friends heard it, they went out to seize him, for they said, "He is beside himself." [22]And the scribes who came down from Jerusalem said, "He is possessed by Be-el′zebul, and by the prince of demons he casts out the demons." [23]And he called them to him, and said to them in parables, "How can Satan cast out Satan? [24]If a kingdom is divided against itself, that kingdom cannot stand. [25]And if a house is divided against itself, that house will not be able to stand. [26]And if Satan has risen up against himself and is divided, he cannot stand, but is coming to an end. [27]But no one can enter a strong man's house and plunder his goods, unless he first binds the strong man; then indeed he may plunder his house.

28 "Truly, I say to you, all sins will be forgiven the sons of men, and whatever blasphemies they utter; [29]but whoever blasphemes against the Holy Spirit never has forgiveness, but is guilty of an eternal sin"—[30]for they had said, "He has an unclean spirit."

3:10: Mk 5:29, 34; 6:56.   **3:12:** Mk 1:45.   **3:13:** Mt 5:1; Lk 6:12.   **3:14–15:** Mt 10:1.
3:16–19: Mt 10:2–4; Lk 6:14–16; Acts 1:13.   **3:19:** Mk 2:1; 7:17.   **3:20:** Mk 6:31.   **3:21:** Mk 3:31–35; Jn 10:20.
3:22–27: Mt 12:24–29; Lk 11:15–22.   **3:22:** Mt 9:34; 10:25.   **3:27:** Is 49:24–25.   **3:28–30:** Mt 12:31–32; Lk 12:10.

---

the demons know his true identity as God's Son (3:11). Jesus' popular appeal here stands in contrast to 3:6 and the resentment of the Pharisees and Herodians.

📖 **3:14 he appointed twelve:** Jesus spent the entire night in prayer before selecting the apostles (Lk 6:12). ● The number of apostles is symbolic: as the 12 sons of Jacob were representatives of Old Covenant Israel (Gen 49:3–28), so Jesus gathers 12 patriarchs to found his New Covenant people in the Church (Mt 19:28; Rev 21:12–14; CCC 551, 765). **to be sent out:** An apostle is "one who is sent out" as a messenger or emissary (Mt 10:5; CCC 858). See chart below: *The Twelve Apostles*.

[k] Other ancient authorities add *whom also he named apostles.*

3:22 Beelzebul: A pagan god worshiped at Ekron (see Baal-zebub, 2 Kings 1:2–16). The name probably meant "Prince Baal". The scribes use it as a disdainful title for Satan. **by the prince of demons:** It was commonly held that weaker demons could be exorcised by more powerful ones. The scribes wrongfully attribute Jesus' power to the sorcery of Satan, the most powerful demon of all (Mt 9:34; 10:25; CCC 548).

3:24–25 By ascribing the power of Jesus to Satan, the scribes reveal their own collaboration with the devil's **kingdom**. Satan's **house** will fall because Christ will conquer him, not because his demons are weakened by divisions within their own ranks (Heb 2:14; 1 Jn 3:8). See note on Mt 12:25–26.

📖 **3:29 an eternal sin:** The scribes utter blasphemy by attributing to Satan what is actually the work of the Holy

---

The Twelve Apostles (Mk 3)

MATTHEW 10:2–4	MARK 3:16–19	LUKE 6:14–16	ACTS 1:13
Simon Peter	Simon Peter	Simon Peter	Peter
Andrew	James	Andrew	John
James	John	James	James
John	Andrew	John	Andrew
Philip	Philip	Philip	Philip
Bartholomew[1]	Bartholomew	Bartholomew	Thomas
Thomas	Matthew	Matthew	Bartholomew
Matthew	Thomas	Thomas	Matthew
James (of Alphaeus)	James (of Alphaeus)	James (of Alphaeus)	James (of Alphaeus)
Thaddaeus[2]	Thaddaeus	Simon (the Zealot)	Simon (the Zealot)
Simon (the Cananaean)[3]	Simon (the Cananaean)	Judas (of James)	Judas (of James)
Judas Iscariot	Judas Iscariot	Judas Iscariot	――――

[1] **Bartholomew** is also called "Nathanael" in John's Gospel (Jn 1:45–49; 21:2).

[2] The apostle called **Thaddaeus** in Matthew and Mark is the same apostle called **Judas the son of James** in Luke and Acts. Some suggest the name **Thaddaeus** was preferred in certain circles to avoid confusing him with Judas Iscariot, who betrayed Jesus.

[3] The name **Cananaean** is probably derived from an Aramaic term meaning "zealot" (as in Luke and Acts). This title usually refers to Jewish revolutionaries who forcibly resisted the Roman rule and occupation of first-century Palestine.

The True Kindred of Jesus

31 And his mother and his brethren came; and standing outside they sent to him and called him. ³²And a crowd was sitting about him; and they said to him, "Your mother and your brethren *ᶦ* are outside, asking for you." ³³And he replied, "Who are my mother and my brethren?" ³⁴And looking around on those who sat about him, he said, "Here are my mother and my brethren! ³⁵Whoever does the will of God is my brother, and sister, and mother."

The Parable of the Sower

4 Again he began to teach beside the sea. And a very large crowd gathered about him, so that he got into a boat and sat in it on the sea; and the whole crowd was beside the sea on the land. ²And he taught them many things in parables, and in his teaching he said to them: ³"Listen! A sower went out to sow. ⁴And as he sowed, some seed fell along the path, and the birds came and devoured it. ⁵Other seed fell on rocky ground, where it had not much soil, and immediately it sprang up, since it had no depth of soil; ⁶and when the sun rose it was scorched, and since it had no root it withered away. ⁷Other seed fell among thorns and the thorns grew up and choked it, and it yielded no grain. ⁸And other seeds fell into good soil and brought forth grain, growing up and increasing and yielding

thirtyfold and sixtyfold and a hundredfold." ⁹And he said, "He who has ears to hear, let him hear."

Explanation of the Parable

10 And when he was alone, those who were about him with the twelve asked him concerning the parables. ¹¹And he said to them, "To you has been given the secret of the kingdom of God, but for those outside everything is in parables; ¹²so that they may indeed see but not perceive, and may indeed hear but not understand; lest they should turn again, and be forgiven." ¹³And he said to them, "Do you not understand this parable? How then will you understand all the parables? ¹⁴The sower sows the word. ¹⁵And these are the ones along the path, where the word is sown; when they hear, Satan immediately comes and takes away the word which is sown in them. ¹⁶And these in like manner are the ones sown upon rocky ground, who, when they hear the word, immediately receive it with joy; ¹⁷and they have no root in themselves, but endure for a while; then, when tribulation or persecution arises on account of the word, immediately they fall away.ᵐ ¹⁸And others are the ones sown among thorns; they are those who hear the word, ¹⁹but the cares of the world, and the delight in riches, and the desire for other things, enter in and choke the word, and it proves unfruitful. ²⁰But those that were sown upon the good soil are the ones who

---

3:31–35: Mt 12:46–50; Lk 8:19–21.   **4:1–9:** Mt 13:1–9; Lk 8:4–8.   **4:10–12:** Mt 13:10–15; Lk 8:9–10.
4:11: 1 Cor 5:12–13; Col 4:5; 1 Thess 4:12; 1 Tim 3:7.   **4:12:** Is 6:9–10.   **4:13–20:** Mt 13:18–23; Lk 8:11–15.

Spirit (3:22, 30). Their sin is not unforgivable in principle since no sin can place us beyond the reach of God's mercy. However, blasphemy **against the Holy Spirit** is a form of rebellion that is particularly grievous because it blinds people to their own need for forgiveness; in this case, sins are unpardonable when they are not confessed with contrition (CCC 1864). ● The sin against the Holy Spirit was prefigured in the OT when the Israelites fashioned the golden calf (Ex 32:1–6). Instead of giving worship and thanks to Yahweh for their deliverance, they honored as their true redeemer an idol of their own making (Ex 32:4).

3:32 your brethren: Jesus' cousins or related kinsmen (CCC 500). See note on Mt 12:46.

3:35 the will of God: Obedience to the Father is more important than being related to Jesus biologically. Baptized Christians are children of God and brothers and sisters of Jesus through the Holy Spirit (Jn 1:12; Rom 8:29; Heb 2:10–11). Membership in this New Covenant family is maintained through a life conforming to God's will (Mt 7:21). **brother . . . sister . . . mother:** Christ widens the scope of his spiritual family to *include* his disciples, not to exclude his Mother or his biological relatives. See note on Mt 12:50.

4:2 in parables: A teaching method with two purposes. (1) Parables *conceal* Jesus' message from the faithless, so that the stories and scenes from everyday life have no impact on those who react to his claims with opposition and violence. See note on 4:12. (2) Parables also *reveal* the mystery of Jesus' mission to those who believe and embrace his message. In short, the parables draw us into divine mysteries according to the measure and intensity of our faith (4:33; CCC 546). See word study: *Parables* at Mt 13.

4:3–8 The parable of the Sower. Jesus places himself in a long line of OT prophets whose message was received by some but rejected by many (Mt 23:37; Heb 11:32–38). Jesus is the **sower** whose message likewise elicits diverse responses. The condition of the **soil** in each scenario determines one's reaction to Jesus (see CCC 29). Three responses prove unfruitful: those like the **path** are corrupted by Satan (4:15); those like **rocky ground** are hampered by weak and partial commitments to the gospel (4:17); those with **thorns** are entangled in the distractions and concerns of the world (4:19). Jesus' graphic language (**devoured, scorched, choked;** 4:4, 6–7) underscores the opposition facing the gospel. In contrast, the **good soil** is receptive to God's word and yields an abundant harvest (CCC 2707). The imagery in Jesus' parable evokes Is 55:10–13, where Isaiah describes God's word as a powerful and effective force. He cannot sow his divine word without bringing blessing and accomplishing his will.

4:11 To you has been given: Jesus explains his parables to the inner circle of disciples. By instructing them privately, he prepares them for their future role as teachers and stewards of God's mysteries (16:15, 20; 1 Cor 4:1). ● According to Vatican II (*Dei Verbum*, 7), Jesus ensures the transmission of his truth to every age by the Holy Spirit, who guides the Church through the teaching and apostolic succession of bishops (Jn 14:26; 16:13; 2 Tim 2:2) (CCC 888–90).

4:12 see but not perceive: A paraphrase of Is 6:9–10. ● Isaiah was commissioned by the Lord to file a covenant lawsuit against Jerusalem in the eighth century B.C. It was a time when wickedness and injustice were flourishing in Israel despite Yahweh's repeated attempts to reform the people (Is 5:1–30). As a result of persistent rebellion, Israel became blind and deaf to the warnings of the prophets. Isaiah's mission was a dreadful one of preaching judgment upon his wayward generation until destruction and exile would overtake all but a holy

---

ᶦ Other early authorities add *and your sisters.*
ᵐ Or *stumble.*

hear the word and accept it and bear fruit, thirty-fold and sixtyfold and a hundredfold."

A Lamp Is Not Hidden

21 And he said to them, "Is a lamp brought in to be put under a bushel, or under a bed, and not on a stand? [22]For there is nothing hidden, except to be made manifest; nor is anything secret, except to come to light. [23]If any man has ears to hear, let him hear." [24]And he said to them, "Take heed what you hear; the measure you give will be the measure you get, and still more will be given you. [25]For to him who has will more be given; and from him who has not, even what he has will be taken away."

A Parable about Seeds

26 And he said, "The kingdom of God is as if a man should scatter seed upon the ground, [27]and should sleep and rise night and day, and the seed should sprout and grow, he knows not how. [28]The earth produces of itself, first the blade, then the ear, then the full grain in the ear. [29]But when the grain is ripe, at once he puts in the sickle, because the harvest has come."

30 And he said, "With what can we compare the kingdom of God, or what parable shall we use for it? [31]It is like a grain of mustard seed, which, when sown upon the ground, is the smallest of all the seeds on earth; [32]yet when it is sown it grows up and becomes the greatest of all shrubs, and puts forth large branches, so that the birds of the air can make nests in its shade."

The Use of Parables

33 With many such parables he spoke the word to them, as they were able to hear it; [34]he did not speak to them without a parable, but privately to his own disciples he explained everything.

Jesus Calms a Storm on the Sea

35 On that day, when evening had come, he said to them, "Let us go across to the other side." [36]And leaving the crowd, they took him with them, just as he was, in the boat. And other boats were with him. [37]And a great storm of wind arose, and the waves beat into the boat, so that the boat was already filling. [38]But he was in the stern, asleep on the cushion; and they woke him and said to him, "Teacher, do you not care if we perish?" [39]And he awoke and rebuked the wind, and said to the sea, "Peace! Be still!" And the wind ceased, and there was a great calm. [40]He said to them, "Why are you afraid? Have you no faith?" [41]And they were filled with awe, and said to one another, "Who then is this, that even wind and sea obey him?"

Jesus Heals the Gerasene Demoniac

5 They came to the other side of the sea, to the country of the Ger´asenes. [n] [2]And when he had come out of the boat, there met him out of the tombs a man with an unclean spirit, [3]who lived among the tombs; and no one could bind him any more, even with a chain; [4]for he had often been bound with shackles and chains, but the chains he wrenched apart, and the shackles he broke in pieces; and no one had the strength to subdue him. [5]Night and day among the tombs and on the mountains he was always crying out, and bruising himself with stones. [6]And when he saw Jesus from afar, he ran and worshiped him; [7]and crying out with a loud voice, he said, "What have you to do with me, Jesus,

---

4:21: Mt 5:15; Lk 8:16; 11:33.   **4:22:** Mt 10:26; Lk 8:17; 12:2.   **4:23:** Mt 11:15; Mk 4:9.   **4:24:** Mt 7:2; Lk 6:38.
4:25: Mt 13:12; 25:29; Lk 8:18; 19:26.   **4:26–29:** Mt 13:24–30.   **4:30–32:** Mt 13:31–32; Lk 13:18–19.
4:34: Mt 13:34; Jn 16:25.   **4:35–41:** Mt 8:18, 23–27; Lk 8:22–25.
5:1–20: Mt 8:28–34; Lk 8:26–39.   **5:7:** Acts 16:17; Heb 7:1; Mk 1:24.

---

remnant of the people (Is 6:13). Jesus likewise addresses a crooked generation and preaches a message that reaches a remnant of Israel but leaves the rest hardened and unresponsive (Jn 12:37–43; Acts 28:23–28).

4:14–20 Jesus explains the parable to his disciples only when they are "alone" (4:10). The crowd "outside" is not privileged to hear its interpretation (4:11).

4:21–22 A parable about the purpose and function of Jesus' teaching. Although the mystery of the kingdom is temporarily **hidden** and **secret** in parables, its true meaning will eventually be **manifest** and **come to light** (Lk 12:2).

4:26–29 An agricultural parable found only in Mark. Jesus compares the mystery of natural, organic growth to the expansion of the **kingdom of God**. The kingdom will visibly mature like **grain**, but the spiritual forces behind it will remain invisible. The parable of the Leaven in Mt 13:33 elucidates the same mystery. ● *Morally* (St. Gregory the Great, *Hom. in Ezek.* 2, 3), the maturing grain signifies our increase in virtue. First, the seeds of good intentions are sown; these gradually give forth the blade of repentance and ultimately the mature ear of charitable works. When established in virtue, we are made ripe for God's harvest.

4:29 the harvest: The day of God's manifestation and judgment (Jer 51:33; Joel 3:13; Mt 13:39; Rev 14:15).

4:30–32 The parable of the Mustard Seed. It is based on the difference between the **smallest** seed and the **greatest** shrub and depicts how Christ's **kingdom** begins with a small band of disciples and gradually grows into a worldwide Church. ● The imagery Jesus uses to explain this is drawn from OT oracles that describe the dominion of ancient empires. Babylon (Dan 4:10–12), Egypt (Ezek 31:1–6), and Israel (Ezek 17:22–24) were all portrayed as kingdoms that grew into mighty trees. See note on Mt 13:32.

4:35–41 Jesus manifests his divinity by exercising authority over nature. ● According to the OT, God *alone* has the power to subdue the raging seas (Ps 89:9; 93:4; 107:28–29). This biblical background alarms the disciples and prompts their question, **Who then is this . . . ?** (4:41). ● *Morally* (St. Augustine, *Sermo* 51), the episode at sea signifies the drama of the Christian life. All of God's children embark with Christ on a life that is full of dangerous storms, especially attacks from evil spirits and temptations of the flesh. We must learn to trust in Christ daily, since he alone can restrain these forces and bring us to the safe harbor of salvation. See note on Mt 8:23–27.

5:1 Gerasenes: Gerasa is one of the cities of the "Decapolis" (5:20), a confederation of ten cities in NT Palestine. They were predominantly Gentile in population, and most of them were located east of the Jordan River. The presence of "swine" in 5:11 reinforces this Gentile context, since the Jews would never herd animals that God declared unclean (Lev 11:7–8).

---

[n] Other ancient authorities read *Gergesenes*, some *Gadarenes*.

Son of the Most High God? I adjure you by God, do not torment me." [8]For he had said to him, "Come out of the man, you unclean spirit!" [9]And Jesus [o] asked him, "What is your name?" He replied, "My name is Legion; for we are many." [10]And he begged him eagerly not to send them out of the country. [11]Now a great herd of swine was feeding there on the hillside; [12]and they begged him, "Send us to the swine, let us enter them." [13]So he gave them leave. And the unclean spirits came out, and entered the swine; and the herd, numbering about two thousand, rushed down the steep bank into the sea, and were drowned in the sea.

14 The herdsmen fled, and told it in the city and in the country. And people came to see what it was that had happened. [15]And they came to Jesus, and saw the demoniac sitting there, clothed and in his right mind, the man who had had the legion; and they were afraid. [16]And those who had seen it told what had happened to the demoniac and to the swine. [17]And they began to beg Jesus [p] to depart from their neighborhood. [18]And as he was getting into the boat, the man who had been possessed with demons begged him that he might be with him. [19]But he refused, and said to him, "Go home to your friends, and tell them how much the Lord has done for you, and how he has had mercy on you." [20]And he went away and began to proclaim in the Decap′olis how much Jesus had done for him; and all men marveled.

A Girl Restored to Life and a Woman Healed

21 And when Jesus had crossed again in the boat to the other side, a great crowd gathered about him; and he was beside the sea. [22]Then came one of the rulers of the synagogue, Ja′irus by name; and seeing him, he fell at his feet, [23]and begged him,

saying, "My little daughter is at the point of death. Come and lay your hands on her, so that she may be made well, and live." [24]And he went with him.

And a great crowd followed him and thronged about him. [25]And there was a woman who had had a flow of blood for twelve years, [26]and who had suffered much under many physicians, and had spent all that she had, and was no better but rather grew worse. [27]She had heard the reports about Jesus, and came up behind him in the crowd and touched his garment. [28]For she said, "If I touch even his garments, I shall be made well." [29]And immediately the hemorrhage ceased; and she felt in her body that she was healed of her disease. [30]And Jesus, perceiving in himself that power had gone forth from him, immediately turned about in the crowd, and said, "Who touched my garments?" [31]And his disciples said to him, "You see the crowd pressing around you, and yet you say, 'Who touched me?'" [32]And he looked around to see who had done it. [33]But the woman, knowing what had been done to her, came in fear and trembling and fell down before him, and told him the whole truth. [34]And he said to her, "Daughter, your faith has made you well; go in peace, and be healed of your disease."

35 While he was still speaking, there came from the ruler's house some who said, "Your daughter is dead. Why trouble the Teacher any further?" [36]But ignoring [q] what they said, Jesus said to the ruler of the synagogue, "Do not fear, only believe." [37]And he allowed no one to follow him except Peter and James and John the brother of James. [38]When they came to the house of the ruler of the synagogue, he saw a tumult, and people weeping and wailing loudly. [39]And when he had entered, he said to them, "Why do you make a tumult and weep? The child

---

5:20: Mk 7:31.   **5:21–43:** Mt 9:18–26; Lk 8:40–56.   **5:22:** Lk 13:14; Acts 13:15; 18:8, 17.
5:23: Mk 6:5; 7:32; 8:23; Acts 9:17; 28:8.   **5:30:** Lk 5:17.   **5:34:** Lk 7:50; Mk 10:52.   **5:37:** Mk 9:2; 13:3.

5:9 Legion: The term for an armed regiment of nearly 6,000 Roman soldiers. It points to the overwhelming presence of demons in the man and accentuates the intensity of spiritual combat between Jesus and forces of evil. Matthew indicates that two men approached Jesus suffering from demonic possession (Mt 8:28). ● *Allegorically* (St. Bede, *In Marcum*), the demoniac represents the Gentile nations saved by Christ. As pagans, they once lived apart from God amid the tombs of dead works, while their sins were performed in service to demons. Through Christ, the pagans are at last cleansed and freed from Satan's domination.

5:13 into the sea: Biblical symbolism associated with the sea is diverse and flexible. ● According to one tradition, God's enemies arise from the sea in the form of beasts that oppress God's people (Dan 7:1–3; Rev 13:1). Here Jesus reverses the direction of evil by sending the demon-possessed swine back into the sea. Like Pharaoh's army in the OT, God's adversaries are **drowned** in the waters (Ex 14:26–28; 15:1).

5:19 the Lord has done for you: Hints at Jesus' divinity (cf. 2:28; 11:3; 12:37). The parallel text in Lk 8:39 has "God".

5:21–43 Two miracle stories connected chronologically and thematically. Both highlight Jesus' power over physical sickness (5:29, 42) and his favorable response to faith (5:23, 34, 36; CCC 548, 2616). The accounts are also linked by the figure "twelve years", which represents the duration of the woman's illness (5:25) and the age of the young girl (5:42).

5:23 lay your hands on her: Often in the Gospels Jesus responds to the persistent pleas of parents whose children are suffering or in danger (7:25–30; 9:17–27; Mt 17:14–18; Jn 4:46–54). His mercy touches these distressed parents whenever they turn to him in faith. Jesus also displays a deep affection for children (10:13–16; Mt 18:5–6).

5:25 a flow of blood: A condition that makes the woman and everything she touches legally unclean (Lev 15:25–30). This excludes her from full participation in the covenant life of Israel. To the crowd's astonishment, Jesus removes her uncleanness *by* physical contact, not in spite of it. See note on 1:40.

5:37 Peter . . . James . . . John: Three of Jesus' closest disciples, who were also present with him at the Transfiguration (9:2) and in the garden of Gethsemane (14:33). They are likewise the only apostles Jesus renamed: Simon became "Peter", which means "rock", while James and John were called "Boanerges", which means "sons of thunder" (3:16–17).

---

[o] Greek *he.* [p] Greek *him.*
[q] Or *overhearing.* Other ancient authorities read *hearing.*

is not dead but sleeping." [40]And they laughed at him. But he put them all outside, and took the child's father and mother and those who were with him, and went in where the child was. [41]Taking her by the hand he said to her, "Tal´itha cu´mi"; which means, "Little girl, I say to you, arise." [42]And immediately the girl got up and walked; for she was twelve years old. And immediately they were overcome with amazement. [43]And he strictly charged them that no one should know this, and told them to give her something to eat.

The Rejection of Jesus at Nazareth

6 He went away from there and came to his own country; and his disciples followed him. [2]And on the sabbath he began to teach in the synagogue; and many who heard him were astonished, saying, "Where did this man get all this? What is the wisdom given to him? What mighty works are wrought by his hands! [3]Is not this the carpenter, the son of Mary and brother of James and Joses and Judas and Simon, and are not his sisters here with us?" And they took offense [r] at him. [4]And Jesus said to them, "A prophet is not without honor, except in his own country, and among his own kin, and in his own house." [5]And he could do no mighty work there, except that he laid his hands upon a few sick people and healed them. [6]And he marveled because of their unbelief.

And he went about among the villages teaching.

The Mission of the Twelve

7 And he called to him the twelve, and began to send them out two by two, and gave them authority over the unclean spirits. [8]He charged them to take nothing for their journey except a staff; no bread, no bag, no money in their belts; [9]but to wear sandals and not put on two tunics. [10]And he said to them, "Where you enter a house, stay there until you leave the place. [11]And if any place will not receive you and they refuse to hear you, when you leave, shake off the dust that is on your feet for a testimony against them." [12]So they went out and preached that men should repent. [13]And they cast out many demons, and anointed with oil many that were sick and healed them.

The Death of John the Baptist

14 King Herod heard of it; for Jesus' [s] name had become known. Some [t] said, "John the baptizer has been raised from the dead; that is why these powers are at work in him." [15]But others said, "It is Eli´jah." And others said, "It is a prophet, like one of the prophets of old." [16]But when Herod heard of it he said, "John, whom I beheaded, has been raised." [17]For Herod had sent and seized John, and bound him in prison for the sake of Hero´di-as, his brother Philip's wife; because he had married her. [18]For John said to Herod, "It is not lawful for you to have your brother's wife." [19]And Hero´di-as had a grudge against him, and wanted to kill him. But

---

5:41: Lk 7:14; Acts 9:40.   5:43: Mk 1:43–44; 7:36.   6:1–6: Mt 13:53–58; Lk 4:16–30..   6:2: Mk 1:21; Mt 7:28.   6:3: Mt 11:6.   6:5: Mk 5:23; 7:32; 8:23.   6:6: Mt 9:35.   6:7–11: Mt 10:1, 5, 7–11; Lk 9:1–5.   6:7: Lk 10:1.   6:11: Mt 10:14.   6:12–13: Mt 11:1; Lk 9:6.   6:13: Jas 5:14.   6:14–16: Mt 14:1–2; Lk 9:7–9; 9:19; Mt 21:11.   6:17–18: Mt 14:3–4; Lk 3:19–20.

5:39 not dead but sleeping: Biblical writers often speak of "sleep" as a euphemism for biological death (Mt 27:52; Jn 11:11; 1 Cor 15:6). Jesus uses this description to emphasize that the girl's condition is only temporary and reversible. ● *Morally* (St. Bede, *In Marcum*), the girl signifies the young Christian whose heart remains deadened by the world. Christ must clear away the crowds of impure thoughts to revive and strengthen the believer to begin walking in good deeds. Spiritual nourishment for this new life is given through the Eucharist.

5:41 Talitha cumi: One of several Aramaic expressions preserved in Mark (7:11, 34; 14:36; 15:22, 34). He regularly translates these expressions for his non-Jewish readers in Rome.

6:1 his own country: Nazareth, the Galilean village where Jesus was raised (Mt 2:23). Following an earlier incident recorded in Lk 4:16–30, this episode marks the second rejection of Jesus by his kinsfolk.

6:3 brother . . . his sisters: Jesus' cousins or more distant relatives (CCC 500). They are not siblings from the same Virgin Mother. See note on Mt 13:55.

6:4 not without honor: Jesus adapts a common proverb to explain his rejection: like the OT prophets before him, Jesus is persecuted and rejected for preaching the word of the Lord (Mt 5:11–12; Heb 11:32–38). Jesus is often called a prophet in the Gospels (Mt 21:11; Lk 7:16; 13:33; 24:19; Jn 4:19).

6:7–13 Jesus dispatches the Twelve **two by two** as emissaries to the surrounding Galilean towns (Mt 10:5–6). It is his **authority** that empowers their ministry of exorcism, healing, and preaching (Mt 10:1). Their mission is a training exercise for leadership in the Church, when they will be summoned

to embrace evangelical poverty (6:8–9) and to trust in God for daily provisions (6:11). ● *Morally* (St. Gregory the Great, *Hom. in Evan.* 17), Jesus sends out the disciples in pairs to signify that the twin precepts of charity are indispensable for the duty of Christian preaching. Those entrusted with this mission must always exemplify the love of God and neighbor.

6:11 shake off the dust: A symbolic act of judgment for those who reject the apostles' preaching. See note on Mt 10:14.

6:13 anointed with oil: A symbol of healing and a medicinal agent in the ancient world (Is 1:6; Lk 10:34). ● According to the Council of Trent, the sacrament of the Anointing of the Sick is "suggested" by this text (*Sess. 14, chap. 1*). Whether or not this episode marks the formal institution of the sacrament, it is clear the disciples' ministry anticipates its future administration in the life of the Church (Jas 5:14–15; CCC 1511–16).

6:14–29 A narrative "flashback" on past events. Mark recounts this episode to dispel rumors that John the Baptist and Jesus are the same person (6:16; 8:28). John's execution foreshadows both the death of Jesus (9:12; 10:32–34) and the martyrdom of other believers in the early Church (Rev 20:4; CCC 523).

6:14 King Herod: Herod Antipas. After the death of Herod the Great (4/1 B.C.), the Roman Emperor Augustus divided the kingdom in Palestine among three of Herod's sons. Herod Antipas was the son who received the title "tetrarch" (Mt 14:1) and governed the regions of Galilee and Perea until A.D. 39. His brothers Archelaus and Philip were apportioned the remainder of their late father's territory. Since "tetrarch" is not strictly a royal title, the use of "King" here probably reflects popular usage and is not intended literally (Mt 14:9).

6:18 your brother's wife: John the Baptist was imprisoned

---

[r] Or *stumbled.*   [s] Greek *his.*
[t] Other ancient authorities read *he.*

she could not, [20]for Herod feared John, knowing that he was a righteous and holy man, and kept him safe. When he heard him, he was much perplexed; and yet he heard him gladly. [21]But an opportunity came when Herod on his birthday gave a banquet for his courtiers and officers and the leading men of Galilee. [22]For when Hero'di-as' daughter came in and danced, she pleased Herod and his guests; and the king said to the girl, "Ask me for whatever you wish, and I will grant it." [23]And he vowed to her, "Whatever you ask me, I will give you, even half of my kingdom." [24]And she went out, and said to her mother, "What shall I ask?" And she said, "The head of John the baptizer." [25]And she came in immediately with haste to the king, and asked, saying, "I want you to give me at once the head of John the Baptist on a platter." [26]And the king was exceedingly sorry; but because of his oaths and his guests he did not want to break his word to her. [27]And immediately the king sent a soldier of the guard and gave orders to bring his head. He went and beheaded him in the prison, [28]and brought his head on a platter, and gave it to the girl; and the girl gave it to her mother. [29]When his disciples heard of it, they came and took his body, and laid it in a tomb.

Feeding the Five Thousand

30 The apostles returned to Jesus, and told him all that they had done and taught. [31]And he said to them, "Come away by yourselves to a lonely place, and rest a while." For many were coming and going, and they had no leisure even to eat. [32]And they went away in the boat to a lonely place by themselves. [33]Now many saw them going, and knew them, and they ran there on foot from all the towns, and got there ahead of them. [34]As he landed he saw a great throng, and he had compassion on them, because they were like sheep without a shepherd; and he began to teach them many things. [35]And when it grew late, his disciples came to him and said, "This is a lonely place, and the hour is now late; [36]send them away, to go into the country and villages round about and buy themselves something to eat." [37]But he answered them, "You give them something to eat." And they said to him, "Shall we go and buy two hundred denarii *ᵘ* worth of bread, and give it to them to eat?" [38]And he said to them, "How many loaves have you? Go and see." And when they had found out, they said, "Five, and two fish." [39]Then he commanded them all to sit down by companies upon the green grass. [40]So they sat down in groups, by hundreds and by fifties. [41]And taking the five loaves and the two fish he looked up to heaven, and blessed, and broke the loaves, and gave them to the disciples to set before the people; and he divided the two fish among them all. [42]And they all ate and were satisfied. [43]And they took up twelve baskets full of broken pieces and of the fish. [44]And those who ate the loaves were five thousand men.

Jesus Walks on the Sea

45 Immediately he made his disciples get into the boat and go before him to the other side, to Beth-sa'ida, while he dismissed the crowd. [46]And after he had taken leave of them, he went into the hills to pray. [47]And when evening came, the boat

---

6:19–29: Mt 14:5–12.   **6:20:** Mt 21:26.   **6:23:** Esther 5:3, 6.   **6:30–31:** Lk 9:10; Mk 3:20.
6:32–44: Mt 14:13–21; Lk 9:11–17; Jn 6:5–13; Mk 8:1–10; Mt 15:32–39.   **6:34:** Mt 9:36.
6:37: 2 Kings 4:42–44.   **6:41:** Mk 14:22; Lk 24:30–31.   **6:45–52:** Mt 14:22–33; Jn 6:15–21.

---

and executed for publicly repudiating the illicit union of Herod Antipas and Herodias, the wife of his half-brother Philip. According to Lev 18:16 and 20:21, the Mosaic Law forbids the union of a man with his brother's wife when the brother is still living. Since Philip was alive and well, the marriage between Antipas and Herodias was no marriage at all—it was adultery. See note on Mt 14:4.

6:23 Whatever you ask me: Herod's oath recalls a similar banquet scene in Esther 5–7. ● Queen Esther was giving a feast for the Persian King Ahasuerus when he promised to grant her any request, even half of his kingdom (Esther 7:1–2). Esther then requested that the king spare the life of the Jews throughout the Persian empire (Esther 7:3–4). This OT scenario is the mirror opposite of Mark's narrative: unlike righteous Esther, the sinful Herodias seizes the opportunity to bid for the execution of a righteous Jew.

6:24 The head of John: The prompt response of Herodias, in light of her "grudge" against John (6:19), suggests his demise was premeditated. The careless oath of Herod Antipas afforded the opportune moment for Herodias to implement her plan (6:26).

6:26 exceedingly sorry: Herod's remorse is overshadowed by his injustice. His reputation before the prestigious company of high officials (6:21) was more important to him than a fair trial and, ultimately, John's life.

6:34 sheep without a shepherd: A familiar simile from the OT. ● It generally depicts Israel's need for spiritual leadership (Num 27:17; 1 Kings 22:17; Jud 11:19; Jer 23:1–3; Zech 10:2). Ultimately God himself promised to shepherd his sheep through the Messiah (Ezek 34:23; Jn 10:11–16).

6:35–44 The miracle of the loaves looks both to the past and to the future. (1) It recalls miraculous feedings from the OT, like the heavenly manna God provided for Israel in the wilderness (Ex 16) and the multiplied loaves and leftover baskets provided by Elisha (2 Kings 4:42–44). (2) It also anticipates the later institution of the Eucharist, where the same string of verbs (taking . . . blessed . . . broke . . . gave) is found together, something that occurs only here and at the Last Supper (14:22; CCC 1335).

6:37 two hundred denarii: A single "denarius" is equivalent to a laborer's daily wage. Over half a year's wages would be required to purchase food for the multitude.

6:41 gave them to the disciples: Jesus does not give the multiplied bread directly to the crowds but distributes it to them by the hands of his apostles. ● This mediation foreshadows their role as New Covenant priests, when they apportion to God's people the heavenly bread that Jesus provides in the Eucharist (CCC 1564).

6:45 Bethsaida: Located on the northern shore of the Sea of Galilee. It is the hometown of Peter, Andrew, and Philip (Jn 1:44; 12:21).

ᵘ The denarius was a day's wage for a laborer.

was out on the sea, and he was alone on the land. ⁴⁸And he saw that they were distressed in rowing, for the wind was against them. And about the fourth watch of the night he came to them, walking on the sea. He meant to pass by them, ⁴⁹but when they saw him walking on the sea they thought it was a ghost, and cried out; ⁵⁰for they all saw him, and were terrified. But immediately he spoke to them and said, "Take heart, it is I; have no fear." ⁵¹And he got into the boat with them and the wind ceased. And they were utterly astounded, ⁵²for they did not understand about the loaves, but their hearts were hardened.

Jesus Heals the Sick in Gennesaret

53 And when they had crossed over, they came to land at Gennes´aret, and moored to the shore. ⁵⁴And when they got out of the boat, immediately the people recognized him, ⁵⁵and ran about the whole neighborhood and began to bring sick people on their pallets to any place where they heard he

was. ⁵⁶And wherever he came, in villages, cities, or country, they laid the sick in the market places, and begged him that they might touch even the fringe of his garment; and as many as touched it were made well.

The Tradition of the Elders

7 Now when the Pharisees gathered together to him, with some of the scribes, who had come from Jerusalem, ²they saw that some of his disciples ate with hands defiled, that is, unwashed. ³(For the Pharisees, and all the Jews, do not eat unless they wash their hands, ᵛ observing the tradition of the elders; ⁴and when they come from the market place, they do not eat unless they purify ʷ themselves; and there are many other traditions which they observe, the washing of cups and pots and vessels of bronze.ˣ) ⁵And the Pharisees and the scribes asked him, "Why do your disciples not live ʸ according to the tradition of the elders, but eat with hands defiled?" ⁶And he said to them,

---

6:48: Mk 13:35.　**6:50:** Mt 9:2.　**6:52:** Mk 8:17.　**6:53–56:** Mt 14:34–36.　**6:56:** Mk 3:10; Mt 9:20.
7:1–15: Mt 15:1–11; Lk 11:38.　**7:4:** Mt 23:25; Lk 11:39.　**7:5:** Gal 1:14.　**7:6–7:** Is 29:13.

6:48 the fourth watch: Between 3 and 6 A.M. The evening hours between 6 P.M. and 6 A.M. were divided into four "watches" (13:35).

ᵛ One Greek word is of uncertain meaning and is not translated.
ʷ Other ancient authorities read *baptize.*
ˣ Other ancient authorities add *and beds.*　ʸ Greek *walk.*

The Places of Jesus' Galilean Ministry

6:50 it is I: Or, "I am". ● Jesus takes for himself the divine name "I AM" that God revealed to Moses at the burning bush (Ex 3:14). This claim to divinity is corroborated as Jesus does what only God can do: he treads upon the sea (Job 9:8). ● *Mystically* (*Glossa ordinaria*), Jesus walks on the water to reveal the mystery of his sinlessness. It is because he is entirely free from the weight of sin that he can stride safely across the sea without sinking.

6:53 Gennesaret: A village on the western shore of the Sea of Galilee.

6:56 the fringe of his garment: Moses instructed the Israelites to wear tassels on their clothing as visible reminders to keep God's commandments (Num 15:38–40). ● Jesus often makes tangible things such as spittle (8:23), clay (Jn 9:6), clothing (5:28–29), and water (Jn 9:7) channels of his healing power. He thus prepares the way for the seven sacraments of the New Covenant, which heal the body and soul as visible instruments of grace (CCC 1504).

7:3 the tradition of the elders: Religious customs manufactured by the Pharisees and added to the Mosaic Law. Sometimes called the oral Law, this body of rituals was designed to supplement God's written Law and intensify its requirements of ritual purity. These traditions were passed on orally until recorded in the Jewish Mishnah about A.D. 200. Here the controversy is sparked by the "unwashed" hands of the disciples (7:2). The Pharisees charge them, not with poor hygiene, but with religious laxity. Jesus responds with a vigorous attack on these Pharisaic customs because they distract practitioners from the more important principles of the Mosaic Law (7:8–9). That is, they emphasize the dangers of ritual impurity (on the hands) to the neglect of moral defilement (in the heart) defined by the commandments (7:20–23). In the end, these traditions promoted by the elders are examples of merely human tradition that the Pharisees have wrongly elevated to an equal level with the revealed Law of God (CCC 581). See note on Col 2:8 and essay: *Who Are the Pharisees?* at Mk 2.

7:6–7 A reference to Is 29:13. ● Isaiah reprimands Jerusalem for consulting its politicians while rejecting the prophets. Because their leaders routinely exclude the Lord from foreign policy decisions and rely instead on their own wisdom, their worship of the Lord has become empty and vain. No longer, says Isaiah, will Yahweh tolerate their lip service when their hearts are devoid of living faith. The Pharisees have fallen into the same trap of rejecting God's wisdom in favor of their own (Mt 23:23; Col 2:20–23). As a result, their venerated

"Well did Isaiah prophesy of you hypocrites, as it is written,

'This people honors me with their lips,
  but their heart is far from me;
7 in vain do they worship me,
  teaching as doctrines the precepts of men.'

[8]You leave the commandment of God, and hold fast the tradition of men."

9 And he said to them, "You have a fine way of rejecting the commandment of God, in order to keep your tradition! [10]For Moses said, 'Honor your father and your mother'; and, 'He who speaks evil of father or mother, let him surely die'; [11]but you say, 'If a man tells his father or his mother, What you would have gained from me is Corban' (that is, given to God) [z] —[12]then you no longer permit him to do anything for his father or mother, [13]thus making void the word of God through your tradition which you hand on. And many such things you do."

14 And he called the people to him again, and said to them, "Hear me, all of you, and understand: [15]there is nothing outside a man which by going into him can defile him; but the things which come out of a man are what defile him." [a] [17]And when he had entered the house, and left the people, his disciples asked him about the parable. [18]And he said to them, "Then are you also without understanding? Do you not see that whatever goes into a man from outside cannot defile him, [19]since it enters, not his heart but his stomach, and so passes on?" [b] (Thus he declared all foods clean.) [20]And he said,

"What comes out of a man is what defiles a man. [21]For from within, out of the heart of man, come evil thoughts, fornication, theft, murder, adultery, [22]coveting, wickedness, deceit, licentiousness, envy, slander, pride, foolishness. [23]All these evil things come from within, and they defile a man."

The Syrophoenician Woman's Faith

24 And from there he arose and went away to the region of Tyre and Sidon.[c] And he entered a house, and would not have any one know it; yet he could not be hidden. [25]But immediately a woman, whose little daughter was possessed by an unclean spirit, heard of him, and came and fell down at his feet. [26]Now the woman was a Greek, a Syrophoeni'cian by birth. And she begged him to cast the demon out of her daughter. [27]And he said to her, "Let the children first be fed, for it is not right to take the children's bread and throw it to the dogs." [28]But she answered him, "Yes, Lord; yet even the dogs under the table eat the children's crumbs." [29]And he said to her, "For this saying you may go your way; the demon has left your daughter." [30]And she went home, and found the child lying in bed, and the demon gone.

Jesus Cures a Deaf Man

31 Then he returned from the region of Tyre, and went through Sidon to the Sea of Galilee, through the region of the Decap'olis. [32]And they brought to him a man who was deaf and had an impediment in his speech; and they begged him to lay his hand upon him. [33]And taking him aside from the multitude privately, he put his fingers into his ears, and he spat and touched his tongue;

7:10: Ex 20:12; Deut 5:16; Ex 21:17; Lev 20:9.   7:17–23: Mt 15:15–20; Mk 4:10.
7:18–19: 1 Cor 10:25–27; Rom 14:14; Tit 1:15; Acts 10:15.   7:20–23: Rom 1:28–31; Gal 5:19–21.   7:22: Mt 6:23; 20:15.
7:24–30: Mt 15:21–28.   7:31–37: Mt 15:29–31.   7:32: Mk 5:23.   7:33: Mk 8:23.

---

traditions are empty and in dangerous competition with God's will as revealed in the gospel.

7:11 Corban: Aramaic for "offering". It denotes something dedicated to God for a religious purpose. It often consisted of money or property donated by vow to the Temple. Jesus denounces the abuse of this practice: giving gifts to the Temple does not exempt children from the obligation of honoring their parents through financial support (Ex 20:12; Deut 5:16; CCC 2218).

7:19 all foods clean: An editorial comment by Mark. Since Jesus traces true defilement back to the heart (7:21), the outward distinctions between clean and unclean as defined by the Old Covenant are no longer operative or binding in the New. These ceremonial distinctions have been superseded in two ways: (1) Ritual defilement was an external matter under the Old Covenant, whereas the New Covenant penetrates to cleanse and govern the inward life of believers (Mt 5:8; Acts 15:9). (2) Since Mosaic food laws effectively separated Israel from the Gentiles, these dietary restrictions were set aside in the New Covenant once Jews and Gentiles were gathered together into the same covenant family. The early Church grappled much with the issues surrounding Old Covenant di-

etary laws and table-fellowship in light of the gospel (Acts 10:9–16; Rom 14:13–23; Gal 2:11–16; CCC 582).

7:21 the heart of man: In biblical terminology, the heart is the center of the person and the source of every decision that manifests itself through deeds. Jesus thus links true defilement with the heart, where evil actions and intentions have their hidden beginning (Mt 5:28). His inventory of vices is similar to others in the NT (Rom 1:29–31; Gal 5:19–21; 1 Pet 4:3; CCC 1432, 2517–19).

7:24 Tyre and Sidon: Two Phoenician cities on the Mediterranean coast, north of Palestine. They were predominantly Gentile in population and thus contemptible to the Jews (Ezek 26:1—28:26; Joel 3:4–8).

7:27 the children first: The children of Israel hold first claim to the blessings of the New Covenant (Mt 15:24; Rom 1:16; 9:4–5; CCC 839). Only after Jesus' Resurrection is the gospel systematically proclaimed to all nations (Mt 28:18–20; Acts 1:8). **dogs:** Often a derogatory term in the Bible (1 Sam 17:43; Phil 3:2; Rev 22:15). Jesus uses it to illustrate the progress of the gospel: just as children are fed before pets, so the gospel is offered to Israel before the Gentiles. The woman's acceptance of this epithet reveals her humility, and her unwillingness to be turned away reveals her perseverance (7:28–29).

7:31 the Decapolis: This setting indicates that Jesus continued to travel and minister in Gentile territory. See note on 5:1.

7:33 privately: Reflects Jesus' intention to conceal his identity. See note on 1:44.

---

[z] Or *an offering.*
[a] Other ancient authorities add verse 16, *"If any man has ears to hear, let him hear".*
[b] Or *is evacuated.*
[c] Other ancient authorities omit *and Sidon.*

³⁴and looking up to heaven, he sighed, and said to him, "Eph′phatha," that is, "Be opened." ³⁵And his ears were opened, his tongue was released, and he spoke plainly. ³⁶And he charged them to tell no one; but the more he charged them, the more zealously they proclaimed it. ³⁷And they were astonished beyond measure, saying, "He has done all things well; he even makes the deaf hear and the mute speak."

Feeding the Four Thousand

8 In those days, when again a great crowd had gathered, and they had nothing to eat, he called his disciples to him, and said to them, ²"I have compassion on the crowd, because they have been with me now three days, and have nothing to eat; ³and if I send them away hungry to their homes, they will faint on the way; and some of them have come a long way." ⁴And his disciples answered him, "How can one feed these men with bread here in the desert?" ⁵And he asked them, "How many loaves have you?" They said, "Seven." ⁶And he commanded the crowd to sit down on the ground; and he took the seven loaves, and having given thanks he broke them and gave them to his disciples to set before the people; and they set them before the crowd. ⁷And they had a few small fish; and having blessed them, he commanded that these also should be set before them. ⁸And they ate, and were satisfied; and they took up the broken pieces left over, seven baskets full. ⁹And there were about four thousand people. ¹⁰And he sent them away; and immediately he got into the boat with his disciples, and went to the district of Dalmanu′tha.ᵈ

The Demand for a Sign

11 The Pharisees came and began to argue with him, seeking from him a sign from heaven, to test him. ¹²And he sighed deeply in his spirit, and said, "Why does this generation seek a sign? Truly, I say to you, no sign shall be given to this generation." ¹³And he left them, and getting into the boat again he departed to the other side.

The Leaven of the Pharisees and of Herod

14 Now they had forgotten to bring bread; and they had only one loaf with them in the boat. ¹⁵And he cautioned them, saying, "Take heed, beware of the leaven of the Pharisees and the leaven of Herod."ᵉ ¹⁶And they discussed it with one another, saying, "We have no bread." ¹⁷And being aware of it, Jesus said to them, "Why do you discuss the fact that you have no bread? Do you not yet perceive or understand? Are your hearts hardened? ¹⁸Having eyes do you not see, and having ears do you not hear? And do you not remember? ¹⁹When I broke the five loaves for the five thousand, how many baskets full of broken pieces did you take up?" They said to him, "Twelve." ²⁰"And the seven for the four thousand, how many baskets full of broken pieces did you take up?" And they said to him, "Seven." ²¹And he said to them, "Do you not yet understand?"

Jesus Cures a Blind Man at Beth-sa′ida

22 And they came to Beth-sa′ida. And some people brought to him a blind man, and begged him to touch him. ²³And he took the blind man by the hand, and led him out of the village; and when he

---

7:36: Mk 1:44; 5:43. 8:1–10: Mt 15:32–39; Mk 6:32–44; Mt 14:13–21; Lk 9:11–17; Jn 6:5–13.
8:11–12: Mt 16:1–4; 12:38–39; Lk 11:29. 8:13–21: Mt 16:4–12. 8:15: Lk 12:1; Mk 6:14; 12:13.
8:17: Mk 6:52; Jer 5:21; Is 6:9–10; Mt 13:10–15. 8:19: Mk 6:41–44. 8:20: Mk 8:1–10.
8:22–26: Mk 10:46–52; Jn 9:1–7. 8:22: Mk 6:45; Lk 9:10. 8:23: Mk 7:33; 5:23.

7:34 Ephphatha: An Aramaic expression that Mark translates for his Gentile readers.
7:37 the deaf . . . the mute: Recalls the messianic blessings prophesied in Is 35:4–6 (Wis 10:21; CCC 549). See note on Mt 11:5.
8:1–10 An episode similar to the miracle in 6:35–44, but dissimilar in several details. Jesus multiplies **seven** (8:5) loaves instead of five (6:38), collects **seven** (8:8) leftover baskets instead of twelve (6:43), and feeds **four thousand** (8:9) people instead of 5,000 (6:44). The symbolism of these figures is examined in 8:18–21.
8:2 I have compassion: The lack of food in this episode illustrates how Jesus rewards the crowd for their perseverance, despite natural discomforts like hunger (8:2).
8:6 given thanks: A translation of the Greek verb *eucharisteō*, which is the basis for the English word "Eucharist." Jesus' multiplication of bread after giving thanks foreshadows the Last Supper and the institution of the Blessed Sacrament (1 Cor 11:24; CCC 1328, 1335). See note on 6:35–44.
8:10 Dalmanutha: An unknown location in Galilee also called "Magadan" (Mt 15:39).
8:11 a sign from heaven: Jesus refuses to perform miracles on demand, especially not for **Pharisees** who are plotting to destroy him (3:6). They are like the Israelites in the wilderness who refused to believe in God, even after seeing numerous signs in Egypt (Num 14:11; CCC 548).

8:15 the leaven: A metaphor based on the "one loaf" in the boat (8:14). Jesus warns the disciples that as leaven permeates and expands bread, so the **Pharisees** and their teaching exert a corruptive influence on the crowds (Mt 16:11–12). Similar imagery is used elsewhere in the NT (Lk 12:1; 1 Cor 5:6–8; Gal 5:9). **Herod:** Herod Antipas, tetrarch of Galilee. He was interested in Jesus primarily as a miracle worker (Lk 23:8). See note on 6:14.
8:19–21 Jesus rehearses the figures in both miracles of the loaves (6:35–44; 8:1–10). While the symbolism of these numbers is nowhere made explicit, they most likely signify the nations who hear the gospel. The **twelve** (8:19) leftover baskets from the first episode represent the twelve tribes of Israel that Jesus gathers into the Church (Mt 15:24; 19:28). The **seven** (8:20) baskets of the second miracle represent the seven Gentile nations who once occupied the land of Canaan alongside Israel (Deut 7:1) and to whom Christ subsequently offers salvation. Jesus' previous conversation with the Syrophoenician (Canaanite) woman in 7:24–30 already established the point that Israel's leftover bread would be given to Gentiles. Together these figures point to the international dimensions of the New Covenant (Rom 1:16; Gal 3:28).
8:22–26 A unique miracle performed in stages. It has multiple significance in Mark: Jesus not only healed the man, but he also heals the spiritual deafness and blindness of the disciples (8:18–21). Although they are still uncertain about his true identity, Jesus sharpens their vision to recognize him as Messiah in the following episode (8:29). ● Allegorically (St.

ᵈ Other ancient authorities read *Magadan* or *Magdala*.
ᵉ Other ancient authorities read *the Herodians*.

had spit on his eyes and laid his hands upon him, he asked him, "Do you see anything?" [24]And he looked up and said, "I see men; but they look like trees, walking." [25]Then again he laid his hands upon his eyes; and he looked intently and was restored, and saw everything clearly. [26]And he sent him away to his home, saying, "Do not even enter the village."

Peter's Declaration That Jesus Is the Christ

27 And Jesus went on with his disciples, to the villages of Caesare´a Philip´pi; and on the way he asked his disciples, "Who do men say that I am?" [28]And they told him, "John the Baptist; and others say, Eli´jah; and others one of the prophets." [29]And he asked them, "But who do you say that I am?" Peter answered him, "You are the Christ." [30]And he charged them to tell no one about him.

Jesus Foretells His Death and Resurrection

31 And he began to teach them that the Son of man must suffer many things, and be rejected by the elders and the chief priests and the scribes, and be killed, and after three days rise again. [32]And he said this plainly. And Peter took him, and began to rebuke him. [33]But turning and seeing his disciples, he rebuked Peter, and said, "Get behind me, Satan! For you are not on the side of God, but of men."

34 And he called to him the multitude with his disciples, and said to them, "If any man would come after me, let him deny himself and take up his cross and follow me. [35]For whoever would save his life will lose it; and whoever loses his life for my sake and the gospel's will save it. [36]For what does it profit a man, to gain the whole world and forfeit his life? [37]For what can a man give in return for his life? [38]For whoever is ashamed of me and of my words in this adulterous and sinful generation, of him will the Son of man also be ashamed, when he comes in the glory of his Father with the holy angels."

8:27–30: Mt 16:13–20; Lk 9:18–21; Jn 6:66–69.　**8:28:** Mk 6:14.　**8:30:** Mk 9:9; 1:34.
8:31—9:1: Mt 16:21–28; Lk 9:22–27.　**8:33:** Mt 4:10.　**8:34:** Mt 10:38; Lk 14:27.
8:35: Mt 10:39; Lk 17:33; Jn 12:25.　**8:38:** Mt 10:33; Lk 12:9.

Bede, *In Marcum*), Jesus heals the blind man to announce the mystery of redemption. As God Incarnate, Jesus heals man through the sacrament of his human nature, here signified by his hands and spittle. This grace cures our spiritual blindness gradually, and, as with the blind man, progress is measured in proportion to our faith. *Allegorically* (St. Jerome, *Homily* 79), the restoration of the blind man signifies our gradual increase in wisdom, from the darkness of ignorance to the light of truth. Christ's spittle is the perfect doctrine that proceeds from his mouth; it enhances our vision and brings us progressively to the knowledge of God.

8:27–10:52 Seven times in this section reference is made to "the way", although this (Greek) motif is muted through various translations like "journey", "road", and "roadside" (8:27; 9:33–34; 10:17, 32, 46, 52). At the narrative level, it depicts the steady movements of Jesus on "the way" to Jerusalem. On a theological level, Jesus is teaching that "the way" to heavenly glory is "the way" of heroic suffering. He first clears "the way" through his own Passion and then summons disciples to follow in his footsteps (1 Pet 2:21; 4:13). ● This Marcan motif recalls the New Exodus motif of Isaiah. Just as Yahweh delivered the Israelites from Egypt and led them on "the way" to the Promised Land (Ex 13:21–22), so Isaiah envisioned a second Exodus from the bondage of sin to a new life with the Lord. The prophet describes this as a great journey along "the way" to Mt. Zion (Is 30:19-21; 35:8-10; 40:3-5; 48:17; 51:10-11; 62:10-11). See note on 1:2-3.

8:27 Caesarea Philippi: A Gentile city beyond the northern border of Palestine. See note on Mt 16:13. **Who do men . . . ?:** Popular opinion agreed that Jesus was a prophet, but there was no consensus about *which* prophet he was (8:28; 6:14-15).

8:29 You are the Christ: i.e., Israel's Messiah and king. Peter's confession is the climax of the first half of Mark's Gospel. To counteract expectations that the Messiah would be a purely political and military figure, Jesus immediately instructs the disciples about the suffering and shame he will have to face to accomplish his mission (8:31-33). See note on Mt 16:16 and word study: *Christ* at Mk 14.

8:30 he charged them: The blessing that accompanied Simon's name change to "Peter" (3:16) is not mentioned in Mark as it is in Matthew (16:17-19). According to one ancient tradition, this omission reflects Mark's dependence upon Peter

for his Gospel information, since it is likely that Peter would humbly omit from his preaching sayings of Jesus that exalt him above others (CCC 552). See note on Mt 16:17 and introduction: *Author.* **tell no one:** Jesus enjoins silence on his disciples as part of a strategy to conceal his "messianic secret". See note on 1:44.

8:31–33 The first of three predictions regarding Jesus' Passion and Resurrection (9:30-32; 10:32-34). In this way Jesus intensifies his effort to instruct the apostles about the suffering that awaits both him and his loyal followers (8:34-37; 13:9).

8:31 the Son of man: Alludes to the royal figure described in Dan 7:13-14. Jesus often associates this title with his Passion (9:12, 31; 10:33, 45; 14:21, 41). See essay: *Jesus the Son of Man* at Lk 17.

8:33 Satan!: Jesus rebukes Peter for rejecting the prospect of suffering. Scandalized and perhaps frightened, Peter briefly aligned himself with the mind-set of Satan, who similarly tried to divert Jesus from his mission to suffer (Mt 4:1-11; Lk 4:1-13). The Crucifixion proved to be a "stumbling block" to many of Jesus' contemporaries (1 Cor 1:23).

8:34 take up his cross: A graphic image of suffering. It refers to the Roman custom of forcing criminals to carry on their shoulders a crossbar to the site of their crucifixion (15:21; Jn 19:17). Jesus warns that disciples must be so committed to him that they are willing to endure persecution, hardship, and even death. The faithful, he assures them, will find resurrection and glory beyond the hardships of this life (Jn 12:24-26; 2 Tim 2:11; CCC 458). See note on Mt 10:38.

8:38 when he comes: The Father has given Christ the authority to judge the living and the dead (Jn 5:22-29; Acts 10:42). At the appointed time he will reward the righteous with eternal life (Rom 2:7) and punish those who are **ashamed** of him with eternal fire (Mt 25:31, 41-46; 2 Tim 2:11-13; CCC 678-79). **with the holy angels:** Jesus alludes to the prophecy of Zech 14:5. ● Zechariah describes the "day of the LORD", when God will bring judgment on the unfaithful of Israel by gathering armies against Jerusalem to plunder the city (Zech 14:1-2). Once the faithful have evacuated the city, God is expected to "come" with his "holy ones" (angels) and there be established "king" over the earth (Zech 14:9). These events transpired with the destruction of Jerusalem in A.D. 70, which

9 And he said to them, "Truly, I say to you, there are some standing here who will not taste death before they see the kingdom of God come with power."

The Transfiguration

2 And after six days Jesus took with him Peter and James and John, and led them up a high mountain apart by themselves; and he was transfigured before them, [3]and his garments became glistening, intensely white, as no fuller on earth could bleach them. [4]And there appeared to them Eli´jah with Moses; and they were talking to Jesus. [5]And Peter said to Jesus, "Master,[f] it is well that we are here; let us make three booths, one for you and one for Moses and one for Eli´jah." [6]For he did not know what to say, for they were exceedingly afraid. [7]And a cloud overshadowed them, and a voice came out of the cloud, "This is my beloved Son;[g] listen to him." [8]And suddenly looking around they no longer saw any one with them but Jesus only.

The Coming of Elijah

9 And as they were coming down the mountain, he charged them to tell no one what they had seen, until the Son of man should have risen from the dead. [10]So they kept the matter to themselves, questioning what the rising from the dead meant. [11]And they asked him, "Why do the scribes say that first Eli´jah must come?" [12]And he said to them, "Eli´jah does come first to restore all things; and how is it written of the Son of man, that he should suffer many things and be treated with contempt? [13]But I tell you that Eli´jah has come, and they did to him whatever they pleased, as it is written of him."

The Healing of a Boy with a Mute Spirit

14 And when they came to the disciples, they saw a great crowd about them, and scribes arguing with them. [15]And immediately all the crowd, when they saw him, were greatly amazed, and ran up to him and greeted him. [16]And he asked them, "What are you discussing with them?" [17]And one of the crowd answered him, "Teacher, I brought my son to you, for he has a mute spirit; [18]and wherever it seizes him, it dashes him down; and he foams and grinds his teeth and becomes rigid; and I asked your disciples to cast it out, and they were not able." [19]And he answered them, "O faithless generation, how long am I to be with you? How long am I to bear with you? Bring him to me." [20]And they brought the boy to him; and when the spirit saw him, immediately it convulsed the boy, and he fell on the ground and rolled about, foaming at the mouth. [21]And Jesus[h] asked his father, "How long

---

9:1: Mk 13:30; Mt 10:23; Lk 22:18.   9:2–8: Mt 17:1–8; Lk 9:28–36.   9:2: Mk 5:37; 13:3.   9:3: Mt 28:3.
9:7: 2 Pet 1:17–18; Mt 3:17; Jn 12:28–29.   9:9–13: Mt 17:9–13; Lk 9:36.   9:9: Mk 8:30; 5:43; 7:36.
9:11: Mt 11:14.   9:12: Mk 8:31; 9:31; 10:33.   9:14–27: Mt 17:14–18; Lk 9:37–43.

---

prefigures the glorious return of Christ at the end of history and the full unveiling of his kingdom.

9:1 not taste death: Jesus promises to inaugurate his **kingdom** within the lifetime of the apostles (1:15). This begins with Christ's heavenly enthronement (16:19) and the birth of the Church. Its authority is manifest with the termination of the Old Covenant, when Jerusalem and the Temple are destroyed with fire (Lk 21:31–32). The kingdom, while present in mystery in the Church, will be fully manifest at the consummation of history (CCC 669–71).

9:2–8 The Transfiguration balances out the shock of Jesus' first Passion prediction in 8:31–33, strengthening the faith of three apostles (9:2) destined for special leadership positions in the early Church. Beholding the glory of Jesus assures them of his divine Sonship and foreshadows their own glorification at the resurrection (CCC 554–55). Like Jesus' Baptism, this event reveals the Trinity: the Father's **voice** is heard (9:7), the Son is **transfigured** (9:2), and the Spirit is present in the **cloud** (9:7). ● *Morally* (Origen, *Comm. in Matt.* 12, 36), Christ led the disciples up the mountain after six days to show that we must rise above our love for created things, which were made by God in six days, to enter on the seventh day into the vision of Christ's glory.

9:2 Peter . . . James . . . John: Three of Jesus' closest companions. See note on 5:37. ● *Anagogically* (Rabanus Maurus, *Comm. in Matt.* 5, 17), Christ took three disciples up the mountain to signify that those who in this life believe in the Holy Trinity will in the next life behold the three Persons of the Godhead in heavenly glory. **high mountain:** Traditionally identified with Mt. Tabor in lower Galilee. Theologically, this mountain is the New Covenant counterpart to Mt. Sinai, where Jesus manifests his divine splendor just as God revealed his glory to

Moses (Ex 24:15–18) and Elijah (1 Kings 19:8–18) on Sinai (Horeb). See note on Mt 17:1–8.

9:4 Elijah with Moses: Representatives of the prophets and the Law of the OT. Together they testify that Jesus is the foretold Messiah and mediator of the New Covenant (cf. Lk 24:25–27; Jn 5:39; Rev 11:3–6).

9:5 three booths: Small shelters in which the Israelites dwelt during the liturgical feast of Booths (Lev 23:39–43). Peter requests to build these shelters in his desire to prolong the heavenly experience.

9:7 listen to him: This final injunction alludes to Deut 18:15. ● Yahweh promised to raise up another prophet like Moses, so that just as Israel received instructions for worship and life issued through Moses, so they must obey the words of his prophetic successor. The Father uses this passage to identify Jesus as this Mosaic prophet (Jn 6:14; Acts 3:22).

9:10 rising from the dead: The belief in a collective resurrection was accepted by many Jews during NT times (Dan 12:2; Jn 11:23–25; Acts 24:15). Only the Sadducees expressly denied it (12:18). The disciples are here perplexed that Jesus speaks of an individual resurrection, since they as yet had no clear understanding of a dying and rising Messiah (8:31–33).

9:11 first Elijah must come: Elijah's reappearance was a common expectation based on the prophecy of Mal 4:5. ● In context, God promised to send Elijah to prepare Israel for his scheduled arrival on the "day of the LORD". His mission was to restore family relationships (Mal 4:6) and the tribes of Israel (Sir 48:10). John the Baptist fulfills this prophetic role as the forerunner to Jesus (9:13). See note on 1:6.

9:13 as it is written of him: As Elijah suffered at the hands of King Ahab and his wife, Jezebel (1 Kings 19:1–10), so John the Baptist suffered martyrdom by Herod Antipas and his mistress Herodias (6:27). See note on 6:14–29.

9:17 a mute spirit: Demon possession is sometimes manifested through sickness, seizures, and self-inflicted injuries (Mt

---

[f] Or *Rabbi.*
[g] Or *my Son, my* (or *the*) *Beloved.*
[h] Greek *he.*

has he had this?" And he said, "From childhood. [22]And it has often cast him into the fire and into the water, to destroy him; but if you can do anything, have pity on us and help us." [23]And Jesus said to him, "If you can! All things are possible to him who believes." [24]Immediately the father of the child cried out [i] and said, "I believe; help my unbelief!" [25]And when Jesus saw that a crowd came running together, he rebuked the unclean spirit, saying to it, "You mute and deaf spirit, I command you, come out of him, and never enter him again." [26]And after crying out and convulsing him terribly, it came out, and the boy was like a corpse; so that most of them said, "He is dead." [27]But Jesus took him by the hand and lifted him up, and he arose. [28]And when he had entered the house, his disciples asked him privately, "Why could we not cast it out?" [29]And he said to them, "This kind cannot be driven out by anything but prayer and fasting." [j]

Jesus Again Foretells His Death and Resurrection

30 They went on from there and passed through Galilee. And he would not have any one know it; [31]for he was teaching his disciples, saying to them, "The Son of man will be delivered into the hands of men, and they will kill him; and when he is killed, after three days he will rise." [32]But they did not understand the saying, and they were afraid to ask him.

True Greatness

33 And they came to Caper′na-um; and when he was in the house he asked them, "What were you discussing on the way?" [34]But they were silent; for on the way they had discussed with one another who was the greatest. [35]And he sat down and called the twelve; and he said to them, "If any one would be first, he must be last of all and servant of all." [36]And he took a child, and put him in the midst of them; and taking him in his arms, he said to them, [37]"Whoever receives one such child in my name receives me; and whoever receives me, receives not me but him who sent me."

Another Exorcist

38 John said to him, "Teacher, we saw a man casting out demons in your name,[k] and we forbade him, because he was not following us." [39]But Jesus said, "Do not forbid him; for no one who does a mighty work in my name will be able soon after to speak evil of me. [40]For he that is not against us is for us. [41]For truly, I say to you, whoever gives you a cup of water to drink because you bear the name of Christ, will by no means lose his reward.

Temptations to Sin

42 "Whoever causes one of these little ones who believe in me to sin,[l] it would be better for him if a great millstone were hung round his neck and he were thrown into the sea. [43]And if your hand causes you to sin,[l] cut it off; it is better for you to enter life maimed than with two hands to go to hell,[m] to the unquenchable fire.[n] [45]And if your foot causes you to sin,[l] cut it off; it is better for you to enter life lame than with two feet to be thrown into hell.[m, n] [47]And if your eye causes you to sin,[l] pluck it out; it is better for you to enter the kingdom of God with

---

9:23: Mt 17:20; Lk 17:6; Mk 11:22–24.   **9:30–32:** Mt 17:22–23; Lk 9:43–45.   **9:31:** Mk 8:31; 10:33.   **9:32:** Jn 12:16.   **9:33–37:** Mt 18:1–5; Lk 9:46–48.   **9:34:** Lk 22:24.   **9:35:** Mk 10:43–44; Mt 20:26–27; 23:11; Lk 22:26.   **9:36:** Mk 10:16.   **9:37:** Mt 10:40; Lk 10:16; Jn 12:44; 13:20.   **9:38–40:** Lk 9:49–50; 11:23; Mt 12:30; Num 11:27–29.   **9:41:** Mt 10:42.   **9:42–48:** Mt 18:6–9; 5:29–30; Lk 17:1–2.

8:16; Mk 1:26; 5:2–5). These phenomena in no way diminish the spiritual dimension of the condition; they simply make it visible. The symptoms here resemble epilepsy (9:18).

9:23 All things are possible: The issue is not whether Jesus *can* cure the boy, but whether his father is willing to believe it. The omnipotent power of God is more than sufficient for the task, but it must be sought with faith and prayer (9:29; Jer 32:17; Lk 1:37). This father, who struggles with "unbelief" (9:24), bids Jesus to stabilize his wavering faith (Lk 17:5; CCC 162, 2610).

9:30–32 Jesus foretells his Crucifixion and Resurrection a second time. The prophecy is still confusing and frightening to the disciples (9:32). See note on 8:31–33.

9:33 Capernaum: Jesus' Galilean residence. See note on 1:21.

9:35 servant of all: Greatness in God's eyes is measured by humility and service to others (Lk 22:24–27), a principle put into practice by Jesus (10:45). As future leaders of the Church, the apostles must shun aspirations for worldly honor and attention in order to serve Christ more faithfully and effectively (8:35; CCC 876, 896).

9:37 one such child: An image of those who are weak and helpless. Welcoming them with affection is tantamount to serving them with Jesus (**me**) and the Father (**him who sent me**). See note on Mt 25:40.

9:42–48 Jesus uses hyperbole (overstatement) to emphasize that drastic measures are needed to avoid sin (CCC 1861, 2284–87). Because public sin can embolden others to sin likewise, the consequences that await those who cause scandal are worse than drowning by the weight of a **great millstone** (9:42). Because grave (mortal) sins merit **hell** (9:43, 45, 47), avoiding them requires us to take action so serious that it can be compared to bodily dismemberment (Mt 5:29–30).
● *Morally* (St. John Chrysostom, *Hom. in Matt.* 59), severing bodily limbs signifies the amputation of intimate friends. When close companions drag Christians away from holiness, they must be cut away. It is better for us to enter heaven without them than to maintain their company in everlasting misery. See word study: *Hell* (page 35).

9:49 salted with fire: Probably a reference to the trials and temptations that face believers. Given the preceding context (9:42–48), it may include the purifying suffering of penance needed to avoid sin and turn away from impure habits. Such fire is meant to test the genuineness of our Christian commitment and lead us to perfection (Sir 2:5; 1 Pet 1:6–7; CCC 1430–31). In the end, those refined by the temporal fires of this world will be spared the unquenchable fires of the next.

---

[i] Other ancient authorities add *with tears.*
[j] Other ancient authorities omit *and fasting.*
[k] Other ancient authorities add *who does not follow us.*
[l] Greek *stumble.*
[m] Greek *Gehenna.*
[n] Verses 44 and 46 (which are identical with verse 48) are omitted by the best ancient authorities.

one eye than with two eyes to be thrown into hell, *m* [48]where their worm does not die, and the fire is not quenched. [49]For every one will be salted with fire. *o* [50]Salt is good; but if the salt has lost its saltiness, how will you season it? Have salt in yourselves, and be at peace with one another."

Teaching about Divorce

10 And he left there and went to the region of Judea and beyond the Jordan, and crowds gathered to him again; and again, as his custom was, he taught them.

[2] And Pharisees came up and in order to test him asked, "Is it lawful for a man to divorce his wife?" [3]He answered them, "What did Moses command you?" [4]They said, "Moses allowed a man to write a certificate of divorce, and to put her away." [5]But Jesus said to them, "For your hardness of heart he wrote you this commandment. [6]But from

the beginning of creation, 'God made them male and female.' [7]For this reason a man shall leave his father and mother and be joined to his wife, *p* [8]and the two shall become one.' *q* So they are no longer two but one. *q* [9]What therefore God has joined together, let not man put asunder."

[10] And in the house the disciples asked him again about this matter. [11]And he said to them, "Whoever divorces his wife and marries another, commits adultery against her; [12]and if she divorces her husband and marries another, she commits adultery."

Jesus Blesses the Children

[13] And they were bringing children to him, that he might touch them; and the disciples rebuked them. [14]But when Jesus saw it he was indignant, and said to them, "Let the children come to me, do not hinder them; for to such belongs the kingdom

---

10:1–12: Mt 19:1–9. **10:1:** Lk 9:51; Jn 10:40; 11:7. **10:4:** Deut 24:1–4. **10:6:** Gen 1:27; 5:2. **10:7–8:** Gen 2:24. **10:11:** Mt 5:32; Lk 16:18; 1 Cor 7:10–11; Rom 7:2–3. **10:13–16:** Mt 19:13–15; 18:3; Lk 18:15–17. **9:48:** Is 66:24. **9:49–50:** Mt 5:13; Lk 14:34–35. **9:50:** Col 4:6; 1 Thess 5:13.

10:1 the region of Judea: Jesus turns from his ministry in Galilee and northern Gentile territory (1:14; 5:1; 7:24; 8:27) to head southward toward Jerusalem (10:32; Lk 9:51). **beyond the Jordan:** Also called Perea, the region governed by Herod Antipas and the location of John the Baptist's ministry (Lk 3:1–3). See note on 6:14 and Mt 19:1.

10:2 to test him: The Pharisees lay a trap for Jesus as part of a strategy to eliminate him (3:6). They anticipate he will deny the legality of **divorce** and so draw upon himself the wrath of Herod Antipas and his unlawful mistress, Herodias. For it was well known that Herod, the ruler of this territory, and his consort had abandoned their spouses in order to remarry. Because John the Baptist had been executed for condemning their unlawful union (6:17–19) as he ministered in this very region

---

m Greek *Gehenna.*
o Other ancient authorities add *and every sacrifice will be salted with salt.*
p Other ancient authorities omit *and be joined to his wife.*
q Greek *one flesh.*

WORD STUDY

Hell (9:43)

Geenna (Gk.): "Gehenna", the valley directly southwest of Jerusalem. Jesus refers to it 11 times in the Gospels as a dreadful symbol of hell. Two associations are made with Gehenna, one drawn from the OT and the other from Jesus' contemporary setting. **(1)** Gehenna is a Greek rendering of the Hebrew place-name "Valley of the sons of Hinnom". It was the site of a frightful Canaanite cult that worshipped the idols of Molech and Baal by burning children in sacrifice (Jer 7:30–32; 19:1–6; 32:35). **(2)** In the NT period, Gehenna served as a smoldering garbage dump where refuse burned continually. Jesus evokes these associations to teach us that hell is not a place of purgation or purification, but one of fiery punishment (Mt 5:22; 18:9; 23:33). In the afterlife, the bodies and souls of the wicked will suffer in hell for eternity (Mt 10:28; 25:41, 46). Other biblical passages corroborate this horrifying prospect (Is 33:14; 66:24; Jude 7; Rev 20:10).

(10:1), the Pharisees hope Jesus will meet the same fate as John by making the same outspoken mistake. See note on 6:18.

10:4 a certificate of divorce: Moses permitted Israelite laymen to divorce their wives under the Old Covenant (Deut 24:1–4). This was a temporary legal concession tailored to the weaknesses of Israel (10:5). Jesus now revokes Mosaic divorce legislation by returning to God's original intention for every married couple: lifelong monogamy (10:6–9). See essay: *Jesus on Marriage and Divorce* at Mt 19. ● Divorce is one of many concessions that Yahweh made for Israel in Deuteronomy. This is seen by a careful reading of the Pentateuch, which distinguishes the Levitical covenant ratified at Mt. Sinai (Ex 19–24; Lev 27:34) from the Deuteronomic covenant that was ratified 40 years later on the plains of Moab (Deut 1:1–5; 29:1). There are, in fact, many laws distinctive to Deuteronomy that are absent in earlier Mosaic legislation: cultic worship was confined to a single, central sanctuary (Deut 12:11), genocidal warfare was permitted for the first time (Deut 20:16–17), animals once sacrificed at the sacred Tabernacle could now be slaughtered in profane contexts (Deut 12:15–24), allowance was made to collect interest on money loaned (Deut 15:3; 23:20), and the grim reality of divorce was tolerated and regulated (Deut 24:1–4). These and other laws indicate that Deuteronomy was a less than perfect law that lowered the standards of covenant faithfulness for wayward Israel (Ezek 20:25). It was always a temporary and concessionary arrangement designed to permit lesser evils in order to avoid greater ones.

10:6 from the beginning: God alone is the Creator of marriage and the laws that govern it. ● Jesus demonstrates this by citing Gen 1:27 and 2:24, passages that describe God's design for marriage as a lifelong union between one man and one woman. This marital bond is spiritual, exclusive, and indissoluble. Since it is forged by God himself (10:9), it cannot be broken by any civil or religious authority (CCC 1603, 1640).

10:11–12 Divorce and remarriage are prohibited in the New Covenant (Lk 16:18; 1 Cor 7:10–11; CCC 2382–86). To divorce and remarry is to commit **adultery**. According to Mark's account, Jesus warns both spouses of this danger. This speaks directly to Mark's readers in ancient Rome, where men and women shared the right to initiate divorce. This double warning may also evoke the well-known story of Herod Antipas' illicit union with Herodias, since *both* of them abandoned their respective spouses before unlawfully remarrying. See note on Mt 14:4 and 19:9.

10:14 Let the children come: When Jesus blesses the children, he attaches great practical importance to his of God. ¹⁵Truly, I say to you, whoever does not receive the kingdom of God like a child shall not enter it." ¹⁶And he took them in his arms and blessed them, laying his hands upon them.

The Rich Man

17 And as he was setting out on his journey, a man ran up and knelt before him, and asked him, "Good Teacher, what must I do to inherit eternal life?" ¹⁸And Jesus said to him, "Why do you call me good? No one is good but God alone. ¹⁹You know the commandments: 'Do not kill, Do not commit adultery, Do not steal, Do not bear false witness, Do not defraud, Honor your father and mother.'" ²⁰And he said to him, "Teacher, all these I have observed from my youth." ²¹And Jesus looking upon him loved him, and said to him, "You lack one thing; go, sell what you have, and give to the poor, and you will have treasure in heaven; and come, follow me." ²²At that saying his countenance fell, and he went away sorrowful; for he had great possessions.

23 And Jesus looked around and said to his disciples, "How hard it will be for those who have riches to enter the kingdom of God!" ²⁴And the disciples were amazed at his words. But Jesus said to them again, "Children, how hard it is for those who trust in riches ʳ to enter the kingdom of God! ²⁵It is easier for a camel to go through the eye of a needle than for a rich man to enter the kingdom of God." ²⁶And they were exceedingly astonished, and said to him,ˢ "Then who can be saved?" ²⁷Jesus looked at them and said, "With men it is impos-

10:16: Mk 9:36. **10:17–31:** Mt 19:16–30; Lk 18:18–30. **10:17:** Lk 10:25; Mk 1:40.
10:19: Ex 20:12–16; Deut 5:16–20. **10:21:** Mt 6:20; Lk 12:33; Acts 2:45; 4:34–35.

teaching on the indissolubility of marriage (10:11–12). Children are, after all, the fruit of married love and the ones who stand most affected by the tragedy of divorce. God intends them to be raised and blessed in the security of a healthy family. ● Jesus welcomes children into the **kingdom of God** and so lays a foundation for the Church's practice of Infant Baptism (CCC 1250–52). See note on Lk 18:16.

10:19 the commandments: Jesus reaffirms the necessity of keeping God's moral laws in the New Covenant (12:28–34; Rom 13:8–10; 1 Cor 7:19). The Ten Commandments forever lead God's children to moral maturity and remain integral to our pursuit of "eternal life" (10:17; CCC 2068, 2072). Jesus cites five precepts of the Decalogue that command us to love our neighbors and parents (Ex 20:2–17; Deut 5:6–21). **do not defraud:** Not an ordinance from the Decalogue but here included with them. It may refer to Deut 24:14.

10:25 easier for a camel: A parable that depicts wealth as a formidable obstacle to entering God's kingdom (1 Tim 6:9–10; Heb 13:5). This difficulty is sorely demonstrated by the young man's refusal to part with his riches and embrace the gospel (10:22). See note on Mt 19:24.

ʳ Other ancient authorities omit *for those who trust in riches.*

10:27 it is impossible: We are completely incapable of reaching salvation on our own. The human family descended from Adam suffers from a wounded nature and is unable to obey God completely or consistently without divine assistance (Rom 7:21–25). Only by cooperating **with God** and his grace can we fulfill the righteous requirements of his Law (Rom 8:4). By our-

The Gospel in a Small Corner

© 1996 Thomas Nelson, Inc.

sible, but not with God; for all things are possible with God." ²⁸Peter began to say to him, "Behold, we have left everything and followed you." ²⁹Jesus said, "Truly, I say to you, there is no one who has left house or brothers or sisters or mother or father or children or lands, for my sake and for the gospel, ³⁰who will not receive a hundredfold now in this time, houses and brothers and sisters and mothers and children and lands, with persecutions, and in the age to come eternal life. ³¹But many that are first will be last, and the last first."

A Third Time Jesus Foretells His Death and Resurrection

32 And they were on the road, going up to Jerusalem, and Jesus was walking ahead of them; and they were amazed, and those who followed were afraid. And taking the twelve again, he began to tell them what was to happen to him, ³³saying, "Behold, we are going up to Jerusalem; and the Son of man will be delivered to the chief priests and the scribes, and they will condemn him to death, and deliver him to the Gentiles; ³⁴and they will mock him, and spit upon him, and scourge him, and kill him; and after three days he will rise."

The Request of James and John

35 And James and John, the sons of Zeb′edee, came forward to him, and said to him, "Teacher, we want you to do for us whatever we ask of you."

³⁶And he said to them, "What do you want me to do for you?" ³⁷And they said to him, "Grant us to sit, one at your right hand and one at your left, in your glory." ³⁸But Jesus said to them, "You do not know what you are asking. Are you able to drink the cup that I drink, or to be baptized with the baptism with which I am baptized?" ³⁹And they said to him, "We are able." And Jesus said to them, "The cup that I drink you will drink; and with the baptism with which I am baptized, you will be baptized; ⁴⁰but to sit at my right hand or at my left is not mine to grant, but it is for those for whom it has been prepared." ⁴¹And when the ten heard it, they began to be indignant at James and John. ⁴²And Jesus called them to him and said to them, "You know that those who are supposed to rule over the Gentiles lord it over them, and their great men exercise authority over them. ⁴³But it shall not be so among you; but whoever would be great among you must be your servant, ⁴⁴and whoever would be first among you must be slave of all. ⁴⁵For the Son of man also came not to be served but to serve, and to give his life as a ransom for many."

Bartimaeus Receives His Sight

46 And they came to Jericho; and as he was leaving Jericho with his disciples and a great multitude, Bartimae′us, a blind beggar, the son of Timae′us, was sitting by the roadside. ⁴⁷And when

---

10:28: Mk 1:16–20. 10:30: Mt 6:33. 10:31: Mt 20:16; Lk 13:30. 10:32–34: Mt 20:17–19; Lk 18:31–34. 10:33: Mk 8:31; 9:12; 9:33. 10:34: Mk 14:65; 15:19, 26–32. 10:35–45: Mt 20:20–28. 10:37: Mt 19:28; Lk 22:30. 10:38: Lk 12:50; Jn 18:11. 10:39: Acts 12:2; Rev 1:9. 10:42–45: Lk 22:25–27. 10:43: Mk 9:35. 10:45: 1 Tim 2:5–6. 10:46–52: Mt 20:29–34; Lk 18:35–43; Mk 8:22–26. 10:47: Mt 9:27.

---

selves we can do nothing (Jn 15:5), but with the Lord's help **all things are possible** (Jer 32:17; Lk 1:37; CCC 2082).

10:33–34 Jesus' third and final prediction of his Passion and Resurrection (8:31–33; 9:30–32). It is the most detailed of the three, specifying that his death will result from a conspiracy of Jewish (**chief priests**, **scribes**) and Roman (**Gentiles**) authorities.

10:38 drink the cup: A reference to Jesus' forthcoming suffering (10:45; 14:36). ● The OT uses this image to depict the misery that God compels the unfaithful to drink (Ps 75:8; Is 51:17; Jer 25:15). Although Jesus is innocent and pure, he consumes the cup that was filled for sinners. **with the baptism:** Symbolic for immersion in trial and suffering. James and John will share in Jesus' cup and baptism as they encounter persecution in the early Church. The NT recounts the martyrdom of James in Acts 12:2 and the exile of John in Rev 1:9.

10:42–45 The ambitions voiced by James and John lead Jesus to clarify the true nature of Christian leadership (10:37). His disciples are not to imitate the pomp and tyranny of Gentile rulers (10:42) but the humility and service he has been modeling for them during his ministry (10:45; Jn 13:14–15; CCC 1551).

10:45 for many: The expression is used idiomatically to mean "for all". It indicates that Jesus will die, not just for some, but for the sins of the entire world (2 Cor 5:14; 1 Jn 2:2). ● Here and elsewhere Jesus interprets his Passion as the fulfillment of the Isaian prophecy about the Suffering Servant (Is 52:13–53:12; Lk 22:37). Pouring out his life "for many" recalls how the messianic Servant will make "many" righteous and remit the sins of "many" by bearing their afflictions (Is 53:11–12; Rom 5:19).

10:46 Jericho: Six miles north of the Dead Sea in the Jordan Valley. Jesus' brief stay in the city was spent with Zacchaeus (Lk 19:1–10).

10:47 Son of David: Refers to the Messiah, who was expected to be a descendant of King David and the rightful heir to his throne (Is 9:7; Ezek 34:23–24). Many hoped he

WORD STUDY

Ransom (10:45)

Lytron (Gk.): a "redemption price" paid for the release of captives. The word occurs only two times in the NT (Mt 20:28; Mk 10:45) but is related to other biblical concepts with a similar meaning (Eph 1:7; 1 Tim 2:5–6). In the OT, kinship relations gave rise to the obligation of protecting one's parents, brothers, sisters, and cousins. Family members thus took responsibility for paying the ransom price for other family members who were taken captive or sold into slavery (Lev 25:47–49). As a divine Father, God became the "Redeemer" of Israel (Is 41:14; 54:5), who ransomed his beloved son from Egypt (Ex 4:22–23; Deut 7:8). In the NT, God purchases his people from slavery in sin (Rom 6:16–18) by the price of Christ's own life (1 Pet 1:18–19). His saving death thus ransomed us for freedom and fellowship in the family of God (1 Cor 6:20; Col 1:11–14; Rev 5:9).

^t Other ancient authorities read *to one another.*

he heard that it was Jesus of Nazareth, he began to cry out and say, "Jesus, Son of David, have mercy on me!" [48]And many rebuked him, telling him to be silent; but he cried out all the more, "Son of David, have mercy on me!" [49]And Jesus stopped and said, "Call him." And they called the blind man, saying to him, "Take heart; rise, he is calling you." [50]And throwing off his cloak he sprang up and came to Jesus. [51]And Jesus said to him, "What do you want me to do for you?" And the blind man said to him, "Master, [t] let me receive my sight." [52]And Jesus said to him, "Go your way; your faith has made you well." And immediately he received his sight and followed him on the way.

Jesus' Entry into Jerusalem

11 And when they drew near to Jerusalem, to Beth´phage and Bethany, at the Mount of Olives, he sent two of his disciples, [2]and said to them, "Go into the village opposite you, and immediately as you enter it you will find a colt tied, on which no one has ever sat; untie it and bring it. [3]If any one says to you, 'Why are you doing this?' say, 'The Lord has need of it and will send it back here immediately.' " [4]And they went away, and found a colt tied at the door out in the open street; and they untied it. [5]And those who stood there said to them,

"What are you doing, untying the colt?" [6]And they told them what Jesus had said; and they let them go. [7]And they brought the colt to Jesus, and threw their garments on it; and he sat upon it. [8]And many spread their garments on the road, and others spread leafy branches which they had cut from the fields. [9]And those who went before and those who followed cried out, "Hosanna! Blessed is he who comes in the name of the Lord! [10]Blessed is the kingdom of our father David that is coming! Hosanna in the highest!"

11 And he entered Jerusalem, and went into the temple; and when he had looked round at everything, as it was already late, he went out to Bethany with the twelve.

Jesus Curses the Fig Tree

12 On the following day, when they came from Bethany, he was hungry. [13]And seeing in the distance a fig tree in leaf, he went to see if he could find anything on it. When he came to it, he found nothing but leaves, for it was not the season for figs. [14]And he said to it, "May no one ever eat fruit from you again." And his disciples heard it.

Jesus Cleanses the Temple

15 And they came to Jerusalem. And he entered the temple and began to drive out those who sold

---

10:52: Mt 9:22; Mk 5:34; Lk 7:50; 8:48; 17:19. **11:1–10:** Mt 21:1–9; Lk 19:29–38. **11:4:** Mk 14:16. **11:7–10:** Jn 12:12–15. **11:9:** Ps 118:26; Mt 21:15; 23:39. **11:11:** Mt 21:10–11, 17. **11:12–14:** Mt 21:18–19; Lk 13:6–9. **11:15–18:** Mt 21:12–16; Lk 19:45–48; Jn 2:13–16.

---

would possess the power to heal sickness and exorcize demons (Mt 15:22), much like the original son of David, King Solomon (Wis 7:20). Here the confession of Bartimaeus is ironic: this blind man sees Jesus' messianic identity more clearly than most people in Mark's Gospel. • *Allegorically* (St. Bede, *In Marcum*), Bartimaeus signifies the Gentile nations saved by Christ. Jesus bids them to rise up from their spiritual blindness, throw aside the mantle of their sinful habits, and follow him down the road to glory. See note on Mt 12:23.

11:1–15:47 Mark devotes over one-third of his Gospel to Passion Week, the final days of Jesus' life. His emphasis on these events reflects their importance for the Church, which annually celebrates them from Palm Sunday to Holy Saturday.

11:1 Jerusalem: Jesus journeys to the Holy City amid thousands of pilgrims arriving for the annual feast of Passover (Ex 12:1–13; CCC 583). It is this OT feast that Jesus transforms at the Last Supper and through his death on the Cross (14:22–25; 1 Cor 5:7). **Bethphage:** Hebrew for "house of figs". Its exact location is uncertain but presumably near **Bethany**, about two miles east of Jerusalem (Jn 11:18). **Mount of Olives:** The mountain directly east of Jerusalem. Its western slope faces the Temple Mount (13:3).

11:7 the colt: Recalls the messianic prophecy of Zech 9:9. • The colt in this oracle symbolizes the king's humility as he comes to Israel in "peace", not mounted on a "war horse" to lead a military strike against Rome (Zech 9:10). Jesus' entry into the city also recalls Solomon's procession into Jerusalem at his coronation as the King of Israel (1 Kings 1:32–40; CCC 559–60). See note on Mt 21:1–11.

11:8–10 Three details surrounding the triumphal entry recall Psalm 118, a psalm chanted by Passover pilgrims flocking to Jerusalem. • (1) The **leafy branches** (11:8) echo the "festal procession with branches" in Ps 118:27. (2) The Hebrew acclamation **Hosanna** (11:9) means "save us" and is taken

from Ps 118:25. (3) **Blessed . . . in the name of the Lord** (11:9) is quoted from Ps 118:26. Jesus later interprets Psalm 118 in the Temple (12:10–11).

11:8 spread their garments: A symbolic gesture for honoring a newly crowned king (2 Kings 9:13). • *Morally* (St. Bede, *In Marcum*), the garments thrown under the colt signify the flesh of Christian martyrs, who lay down their lives for the gospel and so proclaim the Lordship of Jesus Christ.

11:13 a fig tree: A traditional symbol of Israel (Jer 8:13; Hos 9:10). **not the season for figs:** The import of this statement is not immediately clear. It probably underscores what is most evident about Israel: it has yet to bear the fruits of repentance (Lk 13:6–9). When Jesus curses it, the withering and death of the tree become a visible prophecy of the doom that awaits Jerusalem for murdering the Messiah. The same point is made in the following episode, when Jesus topples the commercial stations set up in the Temple.

11:15 to drive out: Animals were sold in the outer court of the Temple as a service to Passover pilgrims who traveled to the city to offer sacrifice. Merchants, however, exploited this arrangement for their own financial gain. According to Jesus, they offended God by *what* they were doing and *where* they were doing it. The Temple should be a house of worship, not a place where daylight thievery and business traffic make prayer impossible. • Jesus' dramatic demonstration of overturning tables foreshadows the Temple's violent destruction in A.D. 70. Several OT passages resonate in the background. (1) His aggressive cleansing of the outer court recalls Mal 3:1–4, where the Lord forewarned Jerusalem that he would make a divine inspection of the Temple to purify the sanctuary and its priests. (2) His temporary interruption of the Temple liturgy (11:16) is a prelude to a more permanent disruption in the sacrificial cult foretold in Dan 9:26–27. (3) His expulsion of the merchants recalls the vision of Zech 14:21, where the prophet predicts that no trader will be found within the Temple precincts in the messianic age. See note on 13:2 and CCC 584.

[t] Or *Rabbi.*

and those who bought in the temple, and he overturned the tables of the money-changers and the seats of those who sold pigeons; [16]and he would not allow any one to carry anything through the temple. [17]And he taught, and said to them, "Is it not written, 'My house shall be called a house of prayer for all the nations'? But you have made it a den of robbers." [18]And the chief priests and the scribes heard it and sought a way to destroy him; for they feared him, because all the multitude was astonished at his teaching. [19]And when evening came they [u] went out of the city.

The Lesson from the Withered Fig Tree

20 As they passed by in the morning, they saw the fig tree withered away to its roots. [21]And Peter remembered and said to him, "Master, [v] look! The fig tree which you cursed has withered." [22]And Jesus answered them, "Have faith in God. [23]Truly, I say to you, whoever says to this mountain, 'Be taken up and cast into the sea,' and does not doubt in his heart, but believes that what he says will come to pass, it will be done for him. [24]Therefore I tell you, whatever you ask in prayer, believe that you receive it, and you will. [25]And whenever you stand praying, forgive, if you have anything against any one; so that your Father also who is in heaven may forgive you your trespasses." [w]

Jesus' Authority Is Questioned

27 And they came again to Jerusalem. And as he was walking in the temple, the chief priests and the scribes and the elders came to him, [28]and they said to him, "By what authority are you doing these things, or who gave you this authority to do them?" [29]Jesus said to them, "I will ask you a question; answer me, and I will tell you by what authority I do these things. [30]Was the baptism of John from heaven or from men? Answer me." [31]And they argued with one another, "If we say, 'From heaven,' he will say, 'Why then did you not believe him?' [32]But shall we say, 'From men'?"—they were afraid of the people, for all held that John was a real prophet. [33]So they answered Jesus, "We do not know." And Jesus said to them, "Neither will I tell you by what authority I do these things."

The Parable of the Wicked Tenants

12 And he began to speak to them in parables. "A man planted a vineyard, and set a hedge around it, and dug a pit for the wine press, and built a tower, and leased it to tenants, and went into another country. [2]When the time came, he sent a servant to the tenants, to get from them some of the fruit of the vineyard. [3]And they took him and beat him, and sent him away empty-handed. [4]Again he sent to them another servant, and they wounded him in the head, and treated him shamefully. [5]And he sent another, and him they killed; and so with many others, some they beat and some they killed. [6]He had still one other, a beloved son; finally he sent him to them, saying, 'They will respect my son.' [7]But those tenants said to one another, 'This is the heir; come, let us kill him, and the inheritance will be ours.' [8]And they took him and killed him, and cast him out of the vineyard. [9]What will the owner of the vineyard do? He will come and destroy the

---

11:17: Is 56:7; Jer 7:11.   11:19: Lk 21:37.   11:20–25: Mt 21:20–22; Mt 17:20; Lk 17:6.   11:24: Jn 14:13–14; 16:23; Mt 7:7–11.   11:25: Mt 6:14–15; 18:35.   11:27–33: Mt 21:23–27; Lk 20:1–8; Jn 2:18.   12:1–12: Mt 21:33–46; Lk 20:9–19; Is 5:1–7.

11:17 house of prayer: A reference to Is 56:7. • Isaiah foresaw Yahweh gathering the Gentiles to share in the covenant worship of Israel. Jesus sees the corruption in the Temple courts as an affront to this oracle (CCC 584). The Temple's outer court—the area reserved for Gentile pilgrims—has become a marketplace where worship is now impossible. Ultimately, Isaiah's vision of a Temple *for* all nations is fulfilled when Jesus makes a Temple *of* all nations in the Church (Eph 2:11–22). **den of robbers:** An excerpt from Jer 7:11. • In context, Jeremiah delivered a sermon in the Temple to warn Israel of God's coming judgment upon Jerusalem. Because Israel failed to repent, Solomon's Temple was destroyed by the Babylonians in 586 B.C. Jesus similarly confronts Israelites who presume that their covenant relationship with God will remain secure despite their sin (Jer 7:8–15). Their impenitence will result in the Temple's second destruction in A.D. 70.

11:23 this mountain: Presumably a reference to Mt. Zion, where Jerusalem stands. Its dramatic removal illustrates the power unleashed through prayer (Mt 17:20; 1 Cor 13:2; CCC 2610). • Jesus may allude to Zech 4:7, where the prophet describes a vision of Zerubbabel rebuilding the Temple after its first destruction (586 B.C.). In his way stood a great mountain that Zerubbabel had to clear away in order to begin construction. Here too the mountain of Jerusalem and the Temple must

be pushed aside to make room for a new Temple: the true house of prayer built of Christian believers quarried from all nations (Mt 16:18; 1 Pet 2:4–5). See note on Mt 24:1–25:46.

11:25 stand praying: A traditional posture for Jewish worship (Ps 134:2; Mt 6:5; Lk 18:11).

11:30 the baptism of John: Jesus questions his interrogators to expose their malice (11:18). If they deny that John's ministry is **from heaven**, they will quickly lose favor with the people (11:32). If they affirm its heavenly authority, they stand condemned for ignoring God's plan for their lives (Mt 21:32; Lk 7:28–30).

12:1–9 The parable of the Wicked Tenants narrates the history of Israel. The story stresses that God has been patient with his wayward people throughout the ages. The **vineyard** represents Israel dwelling in the walled city of Jerusalem (Jer 2:21; Hos 10:1), the **tower** is the Temple (as in Jewish tradition based on Is 5:1–2), and the **tenants** are Israel's leaders stationed in the city. The servants are OT prophets repeatedly sent by God to call for repentance. Many prophets were abused and **killed** (12:5; Lk 13:34). God eventually sent Jesus as the **beloved son** (12:6), whom they also **killed** (12:8). By adding the detail that the son is thrust **out of the vineyard** (12:8), Jesus predicts his Crucifixion outside the city walls of Jerusalem (Jn 19:20). God will avenge his Son when he sends him to **destroy** (12:9) the unfaithful of Jerusalem in A.D. 70. See note on 13:2. • *Morally* (St. Bede, *In Marcum*), the vineyard of Israel signifies every Christian, whose duty it is to cultivate his new life given in Baptism. The Law, the Prophets, and

---

[u] Other ancient authorities read *he.*
[v] Or *Rabbi.*
[w] Other ancient authorities add verse 26, *"But if you do not forgive, neither will your Father who is in heaven forgive your trespasses".*

tenants, and give the vineyard to others. [10]Have you not read this scripture:

'The very stone which the builders rejected
has become the head of the corner;
[11] this was the Lord's doing,
and it is marvelous in our eyes'?"

12 And they tried to arrest him, but feared the multitude, for they perceived that he had told the parable against them; so they left him and went away.

The Question about Paying Taxes

13 And they sent to him some of the Pharisees and some of the Hero´dians, to entrap him in his talk. [14]And they came and said to him, "Teacher, we know that you are true, and care for no man; for you do not regard the position of men, but truly teach the way of God. Is it lawful to pay taxes to Caesar, or not? [15]Should we pay them, or should we not?" But knowing their hypocrisy, he said to them, "Why put me to the test? Bring me a coin, [x] and let me look at it." [16]And they brought one. And he said to them, "Whose likeness and inscription is this?" They said to him, "Caesar's." [17]Jesus said to them, "Render to Caesar the things that are Caesar's, and to God the things that are God's." And they were amazed at him.

The Question about Man's Resurrection

18 And Sad´ducees came to him, who say that there is no resurrection; and they asked him a question, saying, [19]"Teacher, Moses wrote for us that if a man's brother dies and leaves a wife, but leaves no child, the man [y] must take the wife, and raise up children for his brother. [20]There were seven brothers; the first took a wife, and when he died left no children; [21]and the second took her, and died, leaving no children; and the third likewise; [22]and the seven left no children. Last of all the woman also died. [23]In the resurrection whose wife will she be? For the seven had her as wife."

24 Jesus said to them, "Is not this why you are wrong, that you know neither the scriptures nor the power of God? [25]For when they rise from the dead, they neither marry nor are given in marriage, but are like angels in heaven. [26]And as for the dead being raised, have you not read in the book of Moses, in the passage about the bush, how God said to him, 'I am the God of Abraham, and the God of Isaac, and the God of Jacob'? [27]He is not God of the dead, but of the living; you are quite wrong."

The First Commandment

28 And one of the scribes came up and heard them disputing with one another, and seeing that he answered them well, asked him, "Which com-

---

12:10–11: Ps 118:22–23; Acts 4:11; 1 Pet 2:7.   **12:12:** Mk 11:18.   **12:13–17:** Mt 22:15–22; Lk 20:20–26.
12:13: Mk 3:6; Lk 11:54.   **12:17:** Rom 13:7.   **12:18–27:** Mt 22:23–33; Lk 20:27–38.
12:19: Deut 25:5.   **12:26:** Ex 3:6.

---

the Psalms are sent as messengers one after another, and finally, as recounted in the Gospels, the Father sends his Son. Should we despise these servants in pride, and even spurn the Son of God through sin, the graces we forfeit will be given to others more willing to receive them.

12:10–11 A citation from Ps 118:22–23, a psalm chanted by Passover pilgrims flocking to Jerusalem. • Psalm 118 foretells the bitter irony of Holy Week: Jerusalem's leaders (**the builders**) will reject their Messiah (**stone**) despite his divine mission (**the Lord's doing**), while his work will be called **marvelous** by those who recognize him with the **eyes** of faith. The psalm is implying that the old Temple will be replaced with another, where the rejected Messiah will serve as the honored cornerstone of the new edifice (Eph 2:19–22; 1 Pet 2:4–5; CCC 756). See note on 11:8–10.

12:13 Pharisees . . . Herodians: Two opposing groups within ancient Judaism. They stand far apart in their political outlook but close together in their opposition to Jesus (3:6). The Pharisees opposed the Roman rule and occupation of Palestine, whereas the Herodians were sympathetic to Rome's government of Israel through the Herodian dynasty. See essay: *Who Are the Pharisees?* at Mk 2. **entrap him:** Roman taxation was a sensitive and potentially explosive issue for Jews of the NT period. Jesus' opponents thus confront him on the tax in order to trap and eliminate him once and for all. The dilemma they pose appears inescapable: If Jesus agrees with the tax, he will lose credibility with the majority of Jews embittered by Roman rule; if Jesus rejects the tax, he will be reported to the Roman governor on charges of treason.

12:16 Whose likeness . . . ? Jesus responds with a riddle that plays on the word "likeness". Because Caesar's likeness is stamped on the coin for the tax, it should be given back to him as his rightful property. God's image and likeness, however, is

stamped into every living person, including Caesar (Gen 1:27). Even more important than civil responsibilities is the obligation everyone, including Caesar, has to give himself back to God. In the end, Jesus is able to rise above the controversy over taxation by stressing this higher duty incumbent upon all (CCC 450). See note on Mt 22:19.

12:18 Sadducees: Priestly aristocrats who managed the affairs of the Jerusalem Temple. Their denial of a future **resurrection** was unacceptable to most Jews of the day (Acts 23:8; CCC 992–93). Here they consider a future resurrection only hypothetically; they are really out to prove there is no such thing. See topical essay: *Who Are the Sadducees?*

12:19 if a man's brother dies: The Sadducees draw attention to the levirate law of Deut 25:5–6. • This law required a man to marry his brother's widow if the brother died childless (Gen 38:6–8). The man would thus produce children for his deceased brother and carry on his family name in Israel. The Sadducees considered this legislation inconsistent with a belief in bodily resurrection, since the widow's numerous marriages would only lead to confusion if all of her husbands were raised.

12:25 when they rise: At the general resurrection the righteous will become **like angels** in glory and immortality; they will not, however, live as disembodied spirits. Marriage will no longer exist in this state since its purposes are fulfilled during earthly life (CCC 1619). See note on Mt 22:30.

12:26 I am the God: Since the Sadducees restricted biblical authority to the Pentateuch, Jesus deliberately draws from the Pentateuch to demonstrate the resurrection (Ex 3:6). • The passage narrates how Yahweh revealed himself to Moses at the burning bush as the God of the deceased patriarchs: **Abraham, Isaac,** and **Jacob.** Their intimacy with God even after death proves the immortality of their souls (Wis 3:1) and so hints at the future resurrection of their bodies (Is 26:19). See note on 12:18.

---

[x] Greek *a denarius.*   [y] Greek *his brother.*

mandment is the first of all?" [29]Jesus answered, "The first is, 'Hear, O Israel: The Lord our God, the Lord is one; [30]and you shall love the Lord your God with all your heart, and with all your soul, and with all your mind, and with all your strength.' [31]The second is this, 'You shall love your neighbor as yourself.' There is no other commandment greater than these." [32]And the scribe said to him, "You are right, Teacher; you have truly said that he is one, and there is no other but he; [33]and to love him with all the heart, and with all the understanding, and with all the strength, and to love one's neighbor as oneself, is much more than all whole burnt offerings and sacrifices." [34]And when Jesus saw that he answered wisely, he said to him, "You are not far from the kingdom of God." And after that no one dared to ask him any question.

A Question about the Christ

35 And as Jesus taught in the temple, he said, "How can the scribes say that the Christ is the son

---

12:28–34: Mt 22:34–40; Lk 20:39–40; 10:25–28.   **12:29:** Deut 6:4.   **12:31:** Lev 19:18; Rom 13:9; Gal 5:14; Jas 2:8.   **12:33:** 1 Sam 15:22; Hos 6:6; Mic 6:6–8; Mt 9:13.   **12:35–37:** Mt 22:41–46; Lk 20:41–44.

12:29–31 Jesus summarizes the teaching of the entire Old Covenant in two commandments. • The greatest is the Shema (Hebrew for "hear!"), taken from Deut 6:4-5. The Israelites considered this passage a summary or creed of their faith in the one God of the universe. The second is taken from Lev 19:18. Together these injunctions to love God and one's neighbor underlie all 613 precepts of the Mosaic Law and especially the Ten Commandments (Ex 20:2-17; Deut 5:6-21). The distillation of Yahweh's revealed Law into two commandments was prefigured by the two stone tablets of the Decalogue (Ex 34:1).

12:33 burnt offerings and sacrifices: The scribe recalls what is often restated in the Scriptures: the moral laws of God are superior to the sacrificial laws of the Temple (1 Sam 15:22; Jud 16:16; Ps 40:6-8; Hos 6:6; Mic 6:6-8). It is implied that drawing close to the New Covenant kingdom means backing away from the Old Covenant Temple (12:34). • The sacrificial system as managed by the Levitical priesthood was not

---

Who Are the Sadducees?

THE Sadducees make brief but memorable appearances in the NT. They are most often cast in a negative light as the adversaries of Jesus and the early Christians. Sadducees seem to have been Jewish conservatives not prone to embrace new ideas or movements. This religious instinct—to cling to the "old ways"—set them at odds with Jesus and the radical claims of the gospel.

Although historical details about the Sadducees in the NT period are fragmentary, the combination of biblical and extrabiblical evidence brings a reasonably focused picture into view. The Sadducees emerged as a religious and political interest group around the second century B.C. Their name is derived from the high priest Zadok, who served under King Solomon (1 Kings 2:35) and whose descendants were granted exclusive rights to minister in Jerusalem (Ezek 40:46). As part of Jewish society's upper class, it is likely that many Sadducees were wealthy and held important positions in the Holy City. Most notably, the Sadducees were closely associated with the Temple and the priesthood (Acts 4:1; 5:17). While not all Sadducees were Levitical priests, many priests aligned themselves with the Sadducees and their agenda for Jewish life. The Sadducees thus held many "official" leadership positions in Old Covenant Judaism and were in charge of maintaining national relations between Israel and Rome. This high profile earned them the support of wealthier citizens, while many lower-class Jews held them in suspicion and even contempt. The masses probably regarded the Sadducees as corrupt.

Controversy surrounding the Sadducees stems from several factors. First, they were notoriously opposed to the Pharisees, a movement held in honor by many Jews. Unlike the Pharisees, the Sadducees sought to maintain the status quo. Their outlook on Jewish life was likely one of tolerance: Live peaceably with the governing Romans, and Judaism will successfully weather the storm of foreign rule. This collided with the Pharisees' perspective that Israel had to separate and purify itself of the Gentiles, even if this meant driving the Romans out. Second, the Sadducees stand out on the Jewish landscape for their emphatic doctrinal denials. Unlike the majority of first-century Jews, the Sadducees expressly denied: (1) an afterlife with rewards and punishments for the righteous and wicked, (2) the immortality of the soul, (3) the resurrection of the body, and (4) the existence of angels or spirits (Acts 23:6-8). At a more fundamental level, the Sadducees denied full authority to any Scripture except the Pentateuch, the first five books of the Bible (Gen–Deut). As a consequence, they opposed every doctrine not explicitly taught within the Pentateuch. This restrictive view of the biblical canon also provided them with one more reason to oppose the Pharisees: the Sadducees repudiated the oral traditions that the Pharisees developed to supplement the books of Moses (Mk 7:1-5).

In the Gospels, Jesus squares off against the Sadducees only once (Mt 22:23-33; Mk 12:18-27; Lk 20:27-38). While Jesus is teaching in the Temple, the Sadducees approach him with a theological puzzle, convinced that the doctrine of the general resurrection is incompatible with the teaching of the Pentateuch (Deut 25:5). If a woman has several husbands during her life, they reason, surely this will cause great marital confusion in the next life. If all of her husbands are raised, whose wife will she be (Mk 12:20-23)? Jesus responds with ingenuity and tact, affirming nearly everything the Sadducees expressly denied. He asserts the existence of *angels* and deliberately cites the Pentateuch (Ex 3:6) to demonstrate that *souls live beyond death* and that their bodies will one day be *raised* (Mk 12:27). «

of David? ³⁶David himself, inspired by ᶻ the Holy
Spirit, declared,

'The Lord said to my Lord,
Sit at my right hand,
till I put your enemies under your feet.'

³⁷David himself calls him Lord; so how is he his
son?" And the great throng heard him gladly.

Jesus Denounces the Hypocrisy of the Scribes

38 And in his teaching he said, "Beware of the
scribes, who like to go about in long robes, and to
have salutations in the market places ³⁹and the best
seats in the synagogues and the places of honor at
feasts, ⁴⁰who devour widows' houses and for a pre-
tense make long prayers. They will receive the
greater condemnation."

The Widow's Offering

41 And he sat down opposite the treasury, and
watched the multitude putting money into the treasury. Many rich people put in large sums. ⁴²And a
poor widow came, and put in two copper coins,
which make a penny. ⁴³And he called his disciples
to him, and said to them, "Truly, I say to you, this
poor widow has put in more than all those who are
contributing to the treasury. ⁴⁴For they all contrib-
uted out of their abundance; but she out of her
poverty has put in everything she had, her whole
living."

The Destruction of the Temple Foretold

13 And as he came out of the temple, one of his
disciples said to him, "Look, Teacher, what
wonderful stones and what wonderful buildings!"
²And Jesus said to him, "Do you see these great
buildings? There will not be left here one stone
upon another, that will not be thrown down."

3 And as he sat on the Mount of Olives opposite
the temple, Peter and James and John and Andrew
asked him privately, ⁴"Tell us, when will this be,
and what will be the sign when these things are all
to be accomplished?" ⁵And Jesus began to say to
them, "Take heed that no one leads you astray.
⁶Many will come in my name, saying, 'I am he!' and
they will lead many astray. ⁷And when you hear of
wars and rumors of wars, do not be alarmed; this
must take place, but the end is not yet. ⁸For nation
will rise against nation, and kingdom against kingdom; there will be earthquakes in various places,
there will be famines; this is but the beginning of
the sufferings.

Persecutions Foretold

9 "But take heed to yourselves; for they will deliver you up to councils; and you will be beaten in
synagogues; and you will stand before governors

12:36: Ps 110:1; Acts 2:34–35; Heb 1:13.　**12:38–40:** Mt 23:5–7; Lk 20:46–47; Lk 11:43.　**12:41–44:** Lk 21:1–4; Jn 8:20.
13:1–37: Mt 24; Lk 21:5–36.　**13:2:** Lk 19:43–44; Mk 14:58; 15:29; Jn 2:19; Acts 6:14.　**13:3:** Mk 5:37; 9:2.
13:4: Lk 17:20.　**13:6:** Jn 8:24; 1 Jn 2:18.　**13:9–13:** Mt 10:17–22.

part of the Mosaic covenant in Ex 19–24 but was imposed
upon the Israelites after they worshipped the golden calf in Ex
32. Originally, the Mosaic covenant was to consist only of the
Ten Commandments (Deut 5:22; Jer 7:22) and a single sacrificial ceremony where Israelites would renounce idolatry once
and for all by slaughtering the very animals they had begun to
worship in Egypt (Ex 24:3–8; Ezek 20:7–8). However, the
golden calf episode in Ex 32 proved that the Israelites were still
attached to their idols and needed a permanent means to eradi-
cate idolatry from the nation. Detailed legislation for priesthood and sacrifice was thus added to Mosaic covenant as
Yahweh's (temporary) solution to this predicament (Ex 25–31,
35–40; Lev 1–27).

12:36 by the Holy Spirit: Jesus affirms the divine
inspiration of Scripture (2 Tim 3:16; 2 Pet 1:20–
21). Although **David** wrote the Psalm, the Holy Spirit authored
divine words of prophecy through him. **declared:** Scripture itself exposes the inadequate understanding of Israel's leaders.
Although the scribes were rightly aware that the Messiah would
be a royal descendant of David (12:35; 2 Sam 7:12–14), they
overlooked the Messiah's lordship over David in Ps 110. This
leaves them with a dangling question: How can David's son
and successor also be David's superior? ● In Ps 110, David foresaw the greatness of the Messiah by calling him **Lord**, a title
associated with Israel's kings (1 Sam 24:6; 26:19; 1 Kings 1:37).
Accordingly, David's successor becomes his superior once the
Davidic heir is crowned and enthroned by the Lord. Jesus stakes
out this royal claim for himself (14:62; 16:19). ● Theological
reflection yields another solution to this puzzle. Jesus is the son
of David in his humanity, and thus David's successor (Lk 1:32;
Rom 1:3), while he is also the divine Son of God, and thus
David's superior Lord (CCC 202, 668).

12:42 copper coins: The smallest unit of currency in circula-
tion. **a penny:** Worth one sixty-fourth a laborer's daily wage.

12:44 out of her poverty: Jesus points to a paradox: the
poor widow (12:42) gave more to the Temple treasury than
the **rich people** (12:41), despite her minuscule donation. Unlike them, she offered to God her whole livelihood with pure
intentions and a generous spirit (2 Cor 9:7).

13:1–37 Commonly called the Olivet Discourse or "Little
Apocalypse", in which Jesus teaches his disciples at length about
the imminent destruction of Jerusalem and the Temple (A.D.
70). This coming catastrophe will mark the expiration of the
Old Covenant and bring God's vengeance on those who have
rejected Jesus as the Messiah. The Temple's demise is also a
prophetic sign of the end of the world (CCC 585–86). See
essay: *End of the World?* at Mt 24.

13:1 what wonderful stones: Herod the Great began rebuilding the Jerusalem Temple about 20 B.C., and the project was
still in progress during Jesus' ministry (Jn 2:20). Several of its
marble stones measured almost 40 feet in length, some weigh-
ing nearly 100 tons. Its massive platform spanned more than
170,000 square yards, and the wall facing the Mount of Olives
to the east towered more than 300 feet in height. To the senses,
the Temple was an impregnable fortress that appeared inde-
structible by every earthly standard.

13:2 one stone upon another: Jesus' words were fulfilled
in A.D. 70, when Roman legions destroyed Jerusalem and
brought the Old Covenant to a dramatic and violent end (Lk
19:41–44). More than one million Jews perished in the catastrophe. ● Jesus forecasts the Temple's doom, much as the OT
prophets predicted the devastation of Solomon's Temple by
the Babylonians in 586 B.C. (Jer 26:6; Mic 3:12).

13:3 Mount of Olives: See note on 11:1. **opposite the
temple:** Jesus symbolizes his opposition to the Temple's corruption by standing over against it. Once sacred and revered, it
had now become a "den of robbers" (11:17).

13:6 Many will come: According to Acts 5:35–39 and
extrabiblical sources, several self-proclaimed Messiahs appeared
in Israel in the first and second centuries A.D.

ᶻ Or *himself, in.*

and kings for my sake, to bear testimony before them. [10]And the gospel must first be preached to all nations. [11]And when they bring you to trial and deliver you up, do not be anxious beforehand about what you are to say; but say whatever is given you in that hour, for it is not you who speak, but the Holy Spirit. [12]And brother will deliver up brother to death, and the father his child, and children will rise against parents and have them put to death; [13]and you will be hated by all for my name's sake. But he who endures to the end will be saved.

The Desolating Sacrilege

14 "But when you see the desolating sacrilege set up where it ought not to be (let the reader understand), then let those who are in Judea flee to the mountains; [15]let him who is on the housetop not go down, nor enter his house, to take anything away; [16]and let him who is in the field not turn back to get a coat. [17]And alas for those who are with child and for those who are nursing in those days! [18]Pray that it may not happen in winter. [19]For in those days there will be such tribulation as has not been from the beginning of the creation which God created until now, and never will be. [20]And if the Lord had not shortened the days, no human being would be saved; but for the sake of the elect, whom he chose, he shortened the days. [21]And then if any one says to you, 'Look, here is the Christ!' or 'Look, there he is!' do not believe it. [22]False Christs and false prophets will arise and show signs and wonders, to lead astray, if possible, the elect. [23]But take heed; I have told you all things beforehand.

The Coming of the Son of Man

24 "But in those days, after that tribulation, the sun will be darkened, and the moon will not give its light, [25]and the stars will be falling from heaven, and the powers in the heavens will be shaken. [26]And then they will see the Son of man coming in clouds with great power and glory. [27]And then he will send out the angels, and gather his elect from the four winds, from the ends of the earth to the ends of heaven.

The Lesson of the Fig Tree

28 "From the fig tree learn its lesson: as soon as its branch becomes tender and puts forth its leaves, you know that summer is near. [29]So also, when you see these things taking place, you know that he is near, at the very gates. [30]Truly, I say to you, this generation will not pass away before all these things take place. [31]Heaven and earth will pass away, but my words will not pass away.

The Necessity for Watchfulness

32 "But of that day or that hour no one knows, not even the angels in heaven, nor the Son, but only the Father. [33]Take heed, watch and pray; [a] for you do not know when the time will come. [34]It is like a man going on a journey, when he leaves home and puts his servants in charge, each with his work,

---

13:11: Jn 14:26; 16:7–11; Lk 12:11–12. **13:13:** Jn 15:21 **13:14:** Dan 9:27; 11:31; 12:11. **13:17:** Lk 23:29. **13:22:** Mt 7:15; Jn 4:48. **13:26:** Mk 8:38; Mt 10:23; Dan 7:13. **13:30:** Mk 9:1. **13:31:** Mt 5:18; Lk 16:17. **13:32:** Acts 1:7. **13:33:** Eph 6:18; Col 4:2. **13:34:** Mt 25:14.

13:10 to all nations: The missionaries of the early Church must spread the good news throughout the Roman Empire and eventually the world. Much of the Roman world was evangelized by the middle of the first century, just before the onset of Jerusalem's judgment in A.D. 70 (Rom 1:8; Col 1:6, 23; 1 Thess 1:8).

13:12 brother . . . father . . . children: The demands of Christian discipleship outweigh even the sacred duties of family unity and loyalty (Lk 14:26). • The scenes of family strife recall Mic 7:6, where the prophet condemns Jerusalem for her rampant injustices (Mic 6:9—7:10). Although families were suffering internal division (Ezek 22:7), Micah assures Israel that the faithful will be vindicated by God. Jesus evokes this oracle to paint a similar portrait of Jerusalem in his own day: disciples may suffer persecution, but they will be vindicated and delivered in **the end** (13:13).

13:14 the desolating sacrilege: A recurrent expression in Dan 9:27, 11:31, and 12:11. • The desolating sacrilege in Daniel refers to the Temple's desecration in 167 B.C. by the villainous Antiochus Epiphanes IV. He sacked the Jerusalem Temple and erected within it an idol of the Greek god Zeus (1 Mac 1:31, 54). According to Jesus, this tragic event prefigures the final profanation of Jerusalem's Temple by the pagan armies of Rome (Lk 21:20). **those . . . in Judea flee:** Jesus forewarns Christians (13:23) to evacuate Jerusalem when its demise draws near (13:29) and to resist every temptation to defend the city. See note on Mt 24:16.

13:19 such tribulation: Great calamities will precede the Old Covenant's termination (Dan 12:1).

13:24–25 Jesus speaks of cosmic disturbances in the manner of the prophets. • These are not literal predictions of heavenly convulsions or an atmospheric meltdown, but they evoke OT oracles of judgment that foretell the downfall of pagan kingdoms (Is 13:9–10; 34:4; Ezek 32:7-8; Joel 2:10, 31; Amos 8:9). Visions of heavenly chaos serve to underscore the magnitude of God's dreadful judgment, i.e., it will be a "world-shaking" event. Jesus turns the language of these prophecies toward Jerusalem to condemn its pagan ways and forecast its coming doom.

13:26 the Son of man: Jesus identifies himself with the royal figure of Dan 7:13. • Drawing from the details of its original context, Jesus implies that he will be enthroned with the Father and receive a worldwide "kingdom" and "everlasting dominion" (Dan 7:14; Mt 28:18). The oracle foretells his heavenly Ascension (16:19) as well as his Second Coming in glory (Acts 1:11; CCC 673). See essay: *Jesus the Son of Man* at Lk 17.

13:27 the angels: Or, "the messengers". This may denote the apostles and their missionary work (cf. Mk 16:15). See note on Mt 24:31.

13:30 this generation: These words of Jesus were fulfilled with Jerusalem's demise in A.D. 70, within the lifetime of his contemporaries (Mt 10:23; 16:28). His words are thus more reliable than the stable universe itself (13:31). See note on Mt 24:35.

13:32 nor the Son: Jesus describes the general signs preceding Jerusalem's destruction (13:6-23), but does not disclose the exact **day** or **hour** of judgment appointed by the Father (CCC 672-74). See note on Mt 24:36.

13:34 It is like: A short parable to promote vigilance. • *Allegorically* (St. Gregory the Great, *Hom. in Evan.* 9), the parable outlines the responsibilities of the Church before the Second Coming. The man signifies the human nature that Christ assumed in the Incarnation and took into the far country of heaven at his Ascension. Christ then imparts the Holy Spirit

---

[a] Other ancient authorities omit *and pray.*

and commands the doorkeeper to be on the watch. ³⁵Watch therefore—for you do not know when the master of the house will come, in the evening, or at midnight, or at cockcrow, or in the morning—³⁶lest he come suddenly and find you asleep. ³⁷And what I say to you I say to all: Watch."

The Conspiracy to Kill Jesus

14 It was now two days before the Passover and the feast of Unleavened Bread. And the chief priests and the scribes were seeking how to arrest him by stealth, and kill him; ²for they said, "Not during the feast, lest there be a tumult of the people."

The Anointing at Bethany

3 And while he was at Bethany in the house of Simon the leper, as he sat at table, a woman came with an alabaster jar of ointment of pure nard, very costly, and she broke the jar and poured it over his head. ⁴But there were some who said to themselves indignantly, "Why was the ointment thus wasted? ⁵For this ointment might have been sold for more than three hundred denarii,ᵇ and given to the poor." And they reproached her. ⁶But Jesus said, "Let her alone; why do you trouble her? She has done a beautiful thing to me. ⁷For you always have the poor with you, and whenever you will, you can do good to them; but you will not always have me. ⁸She has done what she could; she has anointed my body beforehand for burying.

⁹And truly, I say to you, wherever the gospel is preached in the whole world, what she has done will be told in memory of her."

Judas Agrees to Betray Jesus

10 Then Judas Iscariot, who was one of the twelve, went to the chief priests in order to betray him to them. ¹¹And when they heard it they were glad, and promised to give him money. And he sought an opportunity to betray him.

The Passover with the Disciples

12 And on the first day of Unleavened Bread, when they sacrificed the passover lamb, his disciples said to him, "Where will you have us go and prepare for you to eat the passover?" ¹³And he sent two of his disciples, and said to them, "Go into the city, and a man carrying a jar of water will meet you; follow him, ¹⁴and wherever he enters, say to the householder, 'The Teacher says, Where is my guest room, where I am to eat the passover with my disciples?' ¹⁵And he will show you a large upper room furnished and ready; there prepare for us." ¹⁶And the disciples set out and went to the city, and found it as he had told them; and they prepared the passover.

17 And when it was evening he came with the twelve. ¹⁸And as they were at table eating, Jesus said, "Truly, I say to you, one of you will betray me, one who is eating with me." ¹⁹They began to be sorrowful, and to say to him one after another, "Is it

---

13:35: Lk 12:35–40.   14:1–2: Mt 26:1–5; Lk 22:1–2; Jn 11:47–53.   14:3–9: Mt 26:6–13; Lk 7:36–38; Jn 12:1–8.
14:7: Deut 15:11.   14:8: Jn 19:40.   14:10–11: Mt 26:14–16; Lk 22:3–6.   14:12–16: Mt 26:17–19; Lk 22:7–13.
14:17–21: Mt 26:20–25; Lk 22:14, 21–23; Jn 13:21–30; Ps 41:9.

---

to his servants, enabling them to fulfill their duties in his absence. The pastors of the Church are the doorkeepers, guarding against the intrusion of the devil until Christ's glorious return.

13:35 Watch therefore: The command to be vigilant operates on several levels. (1) The earliest Christians, still worshipping in the Jerusalem Temple (Lk 24:52), must be prepared to flee the city before its downfall (13:14–16). (2) Everyone must be ready for his personal judgment by God (2 Cor 5:10). (3) The Church must persevere in holiness while awaiting Jesus' Second Coming at the end of time (Acts 1:11; 1 Thess 1:10). The Gospels elsewhere focus on similar themes of watchfulness and accountability (14:32–42; Mt 24:45–51; 25:1–13; Lk 19:11–27; CCC 2612, 2849). **evening . . . midnight . . . cockcrow . . . morning:** Names for the four "watches" of the night between 6 P.M. and 6 A.M. See note on 6:48.

14:1 the Passover: The yearly Jewish feast celebrating Israel's deliverance from Egyptian slavery (Ex 12). Pascal lambs (14:12) were sacrificed in the Temple courts the afternoon before the feast. At sundown families or small groups would gather to eat a Seder meal of lamb, unleavened bread, wine, and herbs. Combined with the festival of **Unleavened Bread**, the liturgical celebrations ran seven days, from the 15th of the month (Mar/Apr) until the 21st of the month (Lev 23:4–8; Num 9:1–14). Passover was one of three pilgrim feasts that required Jewish men to travel to Jerusalem (Deut 16:16).

14:2 the people: Jerusalem's normal population of approximately 50,000 swelled to several hundred thousand with the influx of Passover pilgrims. This made the Jerusalem leaders think twice about arresting a popular figure like Jesus, since provoking such unmanageable numbers could easily incite a violent reaction from the Jews and ultimately bring Rome's reprisal upon the city.

14:3 Bethany: See note on 11:1. **a woman came:** According to Jn 12:3, she was Mary, the sister of Martha and Lazarus (Jn 11:1–2). **pure nard:** An aromatic perfume probably imported from India. It is mentioned also in the OT (Song 1:12; 4:13–14).

14:5 three hundred denarii: Equivalent to 300 days' wages. See note on 6:37.

14:7 you always have the poor: Jesus is neither insensitive nor unsympathetic toward the poor. His ministry is marked, rather, by a deep concern for them (Mt 19:21; Lk 4:18; 14:7–14). His words are only meant to underscore the inestimable worth of his presence among the disciples.

14:8 beforehand for burying: It was customary to withhold burial ointments from the bodies of executed criminals. The woman's gesture remedies this deficiency in anticipation of Jesus' impending death as a falsely accused enemy of Rome. See note on Mt 26:12.

14:11 give him money: Judas was given "thirty pieces of silver" (Mt 26:15). His betrayal of Jesus for personal profit contrasts sharply with the woman's generous gift in the preceding episode (14:3–9). Greed blinded Judas from seeing Jesus' true identity and worth.

14:13 a man . . . jar of water: An unusual sight in the context of Jewish culture, since women customarily assumed the task of drawing and carrying water (Gen 24:11; Ex 2:16; Jn 4:7).

14:18 one who is eating with me: According to Matthew and John, Jesus discreetly identifies Judas Iscariot as the traitor (Mt 26:25; Jn 13:26). ● His words allude to Ps 41:9, which foretells the Messiah's betrayal by a close and trusted friend (Jn 13:18).

ᵇ The denarius was a day's wage for a laborer.

I?" ²⁰He said to them, "It is one of the twelve, one who is dipping bread in the same dish with me. ²¹For the Son of man goes as it is written of him, but woe to that man by whom the Son of man is betrayed! It would have been better for that man if he had not been born."

The Institution of the Last Supper

22 And as they were eating, he took bread, and blessed, and broke it, and gave it to them, and said, "Take; this is my body." ²³And he took a cup, and when he had given thanks he gave it to them, and they all drank of it. ²⁴And he said to them, "This is my blood of the ᶜ covenant, which is poured out for many. ²⁵Truly, I say to you, I shall not drink again of the fruit of the vine until that day when I drink it new in the kingdom of God."

Peter's Denial Foretold

26 And when they had sung a hymn, they went out to the Mount of Olives. ²⁷And Jesus said to them, "You will all fall away; for it is written, 'I will strike the shepherd, and the sheep will be scattered.' ²⁸But after I am raised up, I will go before you to Galilee." ²⁹Peter said to him, "Even though they all fall away, I will not." ³⁰And Jesus said to him, "Truly, I say to you, this very night, before the cock crows twice, you will deny me three times."

³¹But he said vehemently, "If I must die with you, I will not deny you." And they all said the same.

Jesus Prays in Gethsemane

32 And they went to a place which was called Gethsem´ane; and he said to his disciples, "Sit here, while I pray." ³³And he took with him Peter and James and John, and began to be greatly distressed and troubled. ³⁴And he said to them, "My soul is very sorrowful, even to death; remain here, and watch."ᵈ ³⁵And going a little farther, he fell on the ground and prayed that, if it were possible, the hour might pass from him. ³⁶And he said, "Abba, Father, all things are possible to you; remove this cup from me; yet not what I will, but what you will." ³⁷And he came and found them sleeping, and he said to Peter, "Simon, are you asleep? Could you not watch ᵈ one hour? ³⁸Watch ᵈ and pray that you may not enter into temptation; the spirit indeed is willing, but the flesh is weak." ³⁹And again he went away and prayed, saying the same words. ⁴⁰And again he came and found them sleeping, for their eyes were very heavy; and they did not know what to answer him. ⁴¹And he came the third time, and said to them, "Are you still sleeping and taking your rest? It is enough; the hour has come; the Son of man is betrayed into the hands of sinners.

14:22–25: Mt 26:26–29; Lk 22:17–19; 1 Cor 11:23–26. 14:22: Mk 6:41; 8:6; Lk 24:30. 14:23: 1 Cor 10:16. 14:24: Ex 24:8; Heb 9:20 14:26–31: Mt 26:30–35; Lk 22:39, 33–34. 14:27: Zech 13:7; Jn 16:32. 14:28: Mk 16:7. 14:30: Mk 14:66–72; Jn 13:36–38; 18:17–18, 25–27. 14:32–42: Mt 26:36–46; Lk 22:40–46; Heb 5:7–8. 14:34: Jn 12:27. 14:36: Rom 8:15; Gal 4:6; Mk 10:38; Jn 18:11. 14:38: Mt 6:13; Lk 11:4.

14:22 took . . . blessed . . . broke . . . gave: Mark uses this same language to recount Jesus' multiplication of the loaves (6:41). See note on 6:35–44. this is my body: Jesus identifies the unleavened bread of the Passover feast with his own flesh (Jn 6:51). This gift of his humanity in the sacrament is inseparable from his self-offering on the Cross (14:24; Heb 10:10), since together they constitute a single sacrifice in which Jesus is both the priest and sacrificial victim of the New Covenant (CCC 1363–65). • Allegorically (St. Bede, In Marcum), Jesus' actions signify the mystery of his Passion. In breaking the bread, Christ pre-enacts the breaking of his body on the Cross. Likewise as Jesus gives himself voluntarily in the Last Supper, so his Crucifixion will be a death he freely accepts, not the end result of hostile forces beyond his control. See note on Mt 26:26–29.

14:24 blood of the covenant: An allusion to Ex 24:8. • As the Old Covenant between Yahweh and Israel was sealed through sacrificial blood on Mt. Sinai, the New Covenant between Christ and the Church is sealed through his own blood poured out in the upper room on Mt. Zion. This new and perfect sacrifice enables us to enter a covenant of communion with the Father through the forgiveness of our sins (Jer 31:31–34; Rom 5:9; Heb 9:22). The blood of Jesus is forever a sacrament of his divine life for those who receive him in the Eucharist (Jn 6:53; CCC 610, 1392–93).

14:26 sung a hymn: Probably Ps 115–118. This was the completion of the Hallel Psalms (113–118) that were sung during the course of the Passover liturgy.

14:27 strike the shepherd: A reference to Zech 13:7. • Zechariah foresaw the messianic shepherd of Israel struck down, leaving his sheep temporarily without leadership. The prophet sees this as a deliberately planned scenario to iden-

tify and purify the faithful of the Lord's flock (Zech 13:8–9). Jesus' arrest sets this time of trial in motion, causing his disciples to scatter in fear (14:49–50).

14:30 before the cock crows: This may refer to the "cockcrow", or third watch of the night, between 12 and 3 A.M. (13:35). Others interpret it more generally to mean "before morning". See note on 6:48. you will deny me: Mark often notes Jesus' foreknowledge of significant events (2:20; 8:31; 10:33–34; 11:1–2; 13:6–9; 14:9).

14:32 Gethsemane: A Hebrew name meaning "oil press". It is a garden area facing Jerusalem on the western slope of the Mount of Olives.

14:36 Abba: An Aramaic word meaning "Father". Jesus uses it to address God the Father and underscore their intimate relationship (Mt 11:27). Paul preserves this title for God in Rom 8:15 and Gal 4:6. • The divine Fatherhood of God is a familiar teaching from the OT, where Yahweh is called the Father of Israel (Deut 32:6; Ps 103:13; Jer 31:9) and the Father of David and his royal successors (2 Sam 7:14; Ps 89:26–27). remove this cup: Jesus fears his impending Passion and Crucifixion (Heb 5:7). See notes on Mt 26:39 and Mk 10:38. what you will: Jesus fully embraced the plan of salvation and so surrendered his human will perfectly and continuously to the Father's divine will (Jn 6:38; 8:29; Phil 2:8).

14:38 into temptation: Prayer and watchfulness are necessary to withstand the attacks of Satan (Col 4:2; 1 Pet 5:8–10). Jesus here refers to man's inner struggle, where the flesh, wounded by sin, is constantly at war with the spirit (Rom 8:12–14; Gal 5:19–24). The graces we need to overcome our weaknesses must be sought through persistent prayer (1 Thess 5:17; Heb 4:16). Although the power of the Holy Spirit enables us to live victoriously, the struggle is not minimized or made easy. God's ready assistance during temptation is also the subject of the final petition of the Lord's Prayer (Mt 6:13; Lk 11:4; CCC 2849).

ᶜ Other ancient authorities insert new.
ᵈ Or keep awake.

⁴²Rise, let us be going; see, my betrayer is at hand."

The Betrayal and Arrest of Jesus

43 And immediately, while he was still speaking, Judas came, one of the twelve, and with him a crowd with swords and clubs, from the chief priests and the scribes and the elders. ⁴⁴Now the betrayer had given them a sign, saying, "The one I shall kiss is the man; seize him and lead him away safely." ⁴⁵And when he came, he went up to him at once, and said, "Master!" *ᵉ* And he kissed him. ⁴⁶And they laid hands on him and seized him. ⁴⁷But one of those who stood by drew his sword, and struck the slave of the high priest and cut off his ear. ⁴⁸And Jesus said to them, "Have you come out as against a robber, with swords and clubs to capture me? ⁴⁹Day after day I was with you in the temple teaching, and you did not seize me. But let the scriptures be fulfilled." ⁵⁰And they all deserted him and fled.

51 And a young man followed him, with nothing but a linen cloth about his body; and they seized him, ⁵²but he left the linen cloth and ran away naked.

Jesus before the Council

53 And they led Jesus to the high priest; and all the chief priests and the elders and the scribes were assembled. ⁵⁴And Peter had followed him at a distance, right into the courtyard of the high priest; and he was sitting with the guards, and warming himself at the fire. ⁵⁵Now the chief priests and the whole council sought testimony against Jesus to put him to death; but they found none. ⁵⁶For many bore false witness against him, and their witness did not agree. ⁵⁷And some stood up and bore false witness against him, saying, ⁵⁸"We heard him say, 'I will destroy this temple that is made with hands, and in three days I will build another, not made with hands.'" ⁵⁹Yet not even so did their testimony agree. ⁶⁰And the high priest stood up in their midst, and asked Jesus, "Have you no answer to make? What is it that these men testify against you?" ⁶¹But he was silent and made no answer. Again the high priest asked him, "Are you the Christ, the Son of the Blessed?" ⁶²And Jesus said, "I am; and you will see the Son of man sitting at the right hand of Power, and coming with the clouds of heaven." ⁶³And the high priest tore his clothes, and said,

---

14:43–50: Mt 26:47–56; Lk 22:47–53; Jn 18:2–11.   **14:49:** Lk 19:47; Jn 18:19–21.
14:53–65: Mt 26:57–68; Lk 22:54–55, 63–71; Jn 18:12–24.   **14:58:** Mk 13:2; 15:29; Acts 6:14; Jn 2:19.
14:62: Dan 7:13; Mk 9:1; 13:26.   **14:63:** Acts 14:14; Num 14:6.

14:45 he kissed him: Normally a gesture of affection in the Bible (Lk 7:45; Rom 16:16; 1 Pet 5:14). Judas Iscariot contorts this kiss into one of betrayal (Prov 27:6).

14:47 Mark leaves both the bearer of the **sword** and the injured **slave** unidentified. It is John who specifies that "Peter" reacted violently with the weapon and identifies the victim as "Malchus" (Jn 18:10). Luke further notes that Jesus healed the man's ear (Lk 22:51).

14:51 a young man: An unnamed witness that many scholars identify as Mark. If this is the case, the evangelist chose to remain anonymous in light of the episode's embarrassing details. Ultimately, how we identify this individual has little bearing on the tradition that Mark wrote the second Gospel as a summary of Peter's preaching, since he could have witnessed the arrest of Jesus without being an eyewitness to his three-year ministry.

14:53 the high priest: Caiaphas, who officiated in Jerusalem from A.D. 18 to 36. While in office, he also presided over the Jewish court, the Sanhedrin. See note on 14:55.

14:55 the whole council: The Sanhedrin, the supreme court of the Jews, which convened in Jerusalem (15:1; Acts 5:27; 23:1). Its origin is traced to the second century B.C., and its primary role was to enforce Jewish law and custom. Fully assembled, the Sanhedrin probably consisted of 71 members: (1) the reigning "high priest", who headed the court, (2) the "elders" of Jerusalem's leading families, (3) "chief priests" who had held the office of high priest, and (4) "scribes", or professional lawyers who were experts in the Law of Moses. Several members were also aligned with the Pharisees or Sadducees (Acts 23:6–10). Under Roman rule, the Sanhedrin retained considerable freedom to regulate the civil and religious affairs of Jewish life. Only the right to administer capital punishment was denied them (Jn 18:31).

14:58 destroy this temple: False witnesses misconstrue the cryptic statements recorded in Jn 2:19 and the Olivet Discourse

(Mt 24:2; Mk 13:2; Lk 21:6). In the former passage Jesus foretold his Resurrection in terms of rebuilding his crucified body, and in the latter context he was predicting the destruction of the Jerusalem Temple. Only shades of his intended meaning filter through this accusation, since Jesus never claimed he would reconstruct the Jerusalem sanctuary after its downfall (13:2). The scandal of the false indictment is twofold: (1) Jesus claims he will erect a new sanctuary in the course of a weekend when the Jerusalem Temple has been at that time 46 years in the making (Jn 2:20), and (2) he claims he will build it without hands, while an army of manual laborers are still at work erecting the existing Temple. See essay: *Made without Hands* at 2 Cor 5.

14:62 I am: Jesus unambiguously accepts the charge that he is the Son of God and the Messiah of Israel. See word study: *Christ*. **the Son of man:** Jesus expects the Father will vindicate him soon after he is condemned. His words evoke the majestic imagery of Ps 110:1 and Dan 7:13. ● The specific contexts of these OT passages are linked together by common images: the Messiah of Ps 110 and the Son of Man in Dan 7 both stand before God in a royal throne room (Ps 110:1; Dan 7:9), and both triumph over their enemies (Ps 110:2, 5–7; Dan 7:23–27). Merging the two texts into a single self-portrait, Jesus claims that God himself will overturn the death sentence of the Sanhedrin by raising him from the dead and enthroning him in glory (CCC 664). See note on Mt 26:64 and essay: *Jesus, the Son of Man* at Lk 17.

14:63 tore his clothes: The Bible often associates this gesture with overwhelming sorrow or distress (Gen 37:29; 2 Kings 19:1; Ezra 9:3). Here the **high priest** disregards the Mosaic Law, which forbids priests to tear their vestments (Lev 10:6; 21:10). ● *Mystically* (St. Bede, *In Marcum*), the drama of Caiaphas tearing his vestments signifies the termination of the Old Covenant priesthood. In contrast, the seamless vestment of Jesus is not torn but remains intact (Jn 19:23–24), signifying that the new priesthood of Christ will endure forever (Heb 7:23–24).

ᵉ Or Rabbi.

"Why do we still need witnesses? [64]You have heard his blasphemy. What is your decision?" And they all condemned him as deserving death. [65]And some began to spit on him, and to cover his face, and to strike him, saying to him, "Prophesy!" And the guards received him with blows.

Peter Denies Jesus

66 And as Peter was below in the courtyard, one of the maids of the high priest came; [67]and seeing Peter warming himself, she looked at him, and said, "You also were with the Nazarene, Jesus." [68]But he denied it, saying, "I neither know nor understand what you mean." And he went out into the gateway.[f] [69]And the maid saw him, and began again to say to the bystanders, "This man is one of them." [70]But again he denied it. And after a little while again the bystanders said to Peter, "Certainly you are one of them; for you are a Galilean." [71]But he began to invoke a curse on himself and to swear, "I do not know this man of whom you speak." [72]And immediately the cock crowed a second time. And Peter remembered how Jesus had said to him, "Before the cock crows twice, you will deny me three times." And he broke down and wept.

Jesus before Pilate

15 And as soon as it was morning the chief priests, with the elders and scribes, and the whole council held a consultation; and they bound Jesus and led him away and delivered him to Pilate. [2]And Pilate asked him, "Are you the King of the Jews?" And he answered him, "You have said so." [3]And the chief priests accused him of many things. [4]And Pilate again asked him, "Have you no answer to make? See how many charges they bring against you." [5]But Jesus made no further answer, so that Pilate wondered.

Pilate Delivers Jesus to Be Crucified

6 Now at the feast he used to release for them one prisoner for whom they asked. [7]And among the rebels in prison, who had committed murder in the insurrection, there was a man called Barab´bas. [8]And the crowd came up and began to ask Pilate to do as he always did for them. [9]And he answered them, "Do you want me to release for you the King of the Jews?" [10]For he perceived that it was out of envy that the chief priests had delivered him up. [11]But the chief priests stirred up the crowd to have him release for them Barab´bas instead. [12]And Pilate again said to them, "Then what shall I do with the man whom you call the King of the Jews?" [13]And they cried out again, "Crucify him." [14]And Pilate said to them, "Why, what evil has he done?" But they shouted all the more, "Crucify him." [15]So Pilate, wishing to satisfy the crowd, released for them Barab´bas; and having scourged Jesus, he delivered him to be crucified.

The Soldiers Mock Jesus

16 And the soldiers led him away inside the palace (that is, the praetorium); and they called together the whole battalion. [17]And they clothed him

---

14:64: Lev 24:16.   **14:66–72:** Mt 26:69–75; Lk 22:56–62; Jn 18:16–18, 25–27; Mk 14:30.   **15:1:** Mt 27:1–2; Lk 23:1; Jn 18:28.
15:2–15: Mt 27:11–26; Lk 23:2–3, 18–25; Jn 18:29—19:16.   **15:11:** Acts 3:14.

---

[f] Or *fore-court*. Other ancient authorities add *and the cock crowed.*

14:64 blasphemy: The Sanhedrin charges Jesus with the capital crime of Lev 24:16. They register his claim to a heavenly enthronement as an insult to God's name. In their eyes, he has no credentials to be Israel's Messiah and king, much less one who will rule the universe in the presence of God (15:32; Jn 10:36).

14:72 the cock crowed: Possibly a bugle call that signaled the end of the third watch (3 A.M.) of the night (13:35). See note on 6:48. **Peter remembered:** He presumably recalled both the prophecy of Jesus (14:30) and his own rash overconfidence (14:31).

15:2 Pilate: Pontius Pilate, the Roman procurator of Judea (A.D. 26–36). He was stationed in Jerusalem for the Passover feast. See note on Mt 27:2. **King of the Jews?:** The Jewish leaders give Jesus a title with obvious political overtones, fully aware that Roman law punishes the crime of treason by death (Lk 23:2; Jn 19:12). The accusation dominates the subsequent narrative (15:9, 12, 18, 26).

15:11 Barabbas: An Aramaic name that literally means "son of the father". Aramaic-speaking Christians surely detected the tragic irony: the guilty Barabbas is released in place of Jesus, the truly innocent Son of the Father (1:1, 11; 3:11; 9:7; 15:39).

15:15 to satisfy the crowd: Pilate remained unconvinced of Jesus' guilt throughout the trial (15:14; Lk 23:4; Jn 19:4). Nevertheless, he lacked the integrity to release Jesus and crumbled instead beneath the pressure of the Jerusalem mob. As the Roman magistrate, Pilate alone had the authority to execute Jesus, since the Jewish leaders were powerless to enforce the penalty of capital punishment without him (Jn 18:31; 19:10; CCC 596–97).

15:16 the praetorium: Pilate's official residence in Jerusalem, built by Herod the Great. **the whole battalion:** A military cohort of up to 600 men.

in a purple cloak, and plaiting a crown of thorns they put it on him. [18]And they began to salute him, "Hail, King of the Jews!" [19]And they struck his head with a reed, and spat upon him, and they knelt down in homage to him. [20]And when they had mocked him, they stripped him of the purple cloak, and put his own clothes on him. And they led him out to crucify him.

The Crucifixion of Jesus

21 And they compelled a passer-by, Simon of Cyre′ne, who was coming in from the country, the father of Alexander and Rufus, to carry his cross. [22]And they brought him to the place called Gol′gotha (which means the place of a skull). [23]And they offered him wine mingled with myrrh; but he did not take it. [24]And they crucified him, and divided his garments among them, casting lots for them, to decide what each should take. [25]And it was the third hour, when they crucified him. [26]And the inscription of the charge against him read, "The King of the Jews." [27]And with him they crucified two robbers, one on his right and one on his left.[g] [29]And those who passed by derided him, shaking

their heads, and saying, "Aha! You who would destroy the temple and build it in three days, [30]save yourself, and come down from the cross!" [31]So also the chief priests mocked him to one another with the scribes, saying, "He saved others; he cannot save himself. [32]Let the Christ, the King of Israel, come down now from the cross, that we may see and believe." Those who were crucified with him also reviled him.

The Death of Jesus

33 And when the sixth hour had come, there was darkness over the whole land [h] until the ninth hour. [34]And at the ninth hour Jesus cried with a loud voice, "E′lo-i, E′lo-i, la′ma sabach-tha′ni?" which means, "My God, my God, why have you forsaken me?" [35]And some of the bystanders hearing it said, "Behold, he is calling Eli′jah." [36]And one ran and, filling a sponge full of vinegar, put it on a reed and gave it to him to drink, saying, "Wait, let us see whether Eli′jah will come to take him down." [37]And Jesus uttered a loud cry, and breathed his last. [38]And the curtain of the temple was torn in two, from top to bottom. [39]And when the centurion, who

---

15:16–20: Mt 27:27–31; Lk 23:11; Jn 19:2–3.   **15:21:** Mt 27:32; Lk 23:26; Rom 16:13.
15:22–32: Mt 27:33–44; Lk 23:33–39; Jn 19:17–24.   **15:24:** Ps 22:18.   **15:29:** Mk 13:2; 14:58; Jn 2:19.   **15:31:** Ps 22:7–8.
15:33–41: Mt 27:45–56; Lk 23:44–49; Jn 19:28–30.   **15:34:** Ps 22:1.   **15:36:** Ps 69:21.
15:38: Heb 10:19–20.   **15:39:** Mk 1:11; 9:7.

15:17–19 The soldier's mockery of Jesus is surrounded with paradox and irony. They remain unaware in their ridicule that Jesus is truly a king (Jn 18:36). Adorning him with a **purple cloak** and a **crown** and kneeling in false **homage**, the soldiers unwittingly bear witness to the royal identity of Jesus (Lk 1:32–33; Rev 19:16).

15:21 they compelled: Roman garrisons in NT Palestine claimed the right to recruit Jews for temporary service (see Mt 5:41). Mark designates **Simon of Cyrene** as the individual forced to assist Jesus. His son **Rufus** may have been a well-known member of the early Roman Church (Rom 16:13).

15:22 Golgotha: The Aramaic word for **skull**. The popular term "Calvary" is derived from the Latin Vulgate translation (Lat. *Calvariae*). Located outside Jerusalem's walls (Jn 19:20), Golgotha may have acquired its name as a common site for criminal executions.

15:23 wine . . . with myrrh: A narcotic painkiller. Jesus refuses it, choosing instead to bear the full weight of suffering for man's sin (Col 1:24; 1 Pet 2:24).

15:24 they crucified him: A form of Roman execution adopted from earlier Persian practice. Crucifixion was torturous, degrading, and reserved for the most heinous criminals—usually insurrectionists. The victims' feet were nailed to an upright stake and their wrists to a wooden crossbeam (Ps 22:16). Death came slowly from a combination of blood loss and asphyxiation, a process that could be hastened by breaking the criminal's legs (Jn 19:33). Corpses were often left hanging for days as a public deterrent against criminal activity and a powerful symbol of Rome's domination of Palestine. ● Christian tradition sees in Jesus' physical death on the tree (Acts 10:39) a reflection of Adam's spiritual death at the tree of good and evil (Gen 3:6, 17–19). Whereas Adam's sin brought death to the entire human family, Jesus' death rescues man from sin and gives him new life in the family of God (Rom 5:12–19). **divided his garments:** The collection of spoil by the execution squad recalls the messianic prophecy of

Ps 22:18. This text is explicitly quoted in Jn 19:24. See note on 15:34.

15:25 the third hour: About 9 A.M. on Friday morning of Passion Week (15:42). See note on Mt 20:1.

15:29 derided him: Literally, "they were blaspheming him". ● By slandering and shaking their heads at Jesus, the angry crowd unwittingly fulfills messianic prophecy from Ps 22:7.

15:33 sixth hour . . . ninth hour: i.e., from noon until 3 P.M. Luke's account may suggest that the **darkness** was caused by an extended solar eclipse (Lk 23:45). ● The OT associates such dreadful darkness with divine judgment on sin (Ex 10:21–23; Is 13:10–11; Amos 8:9). See notes on Mt 20:1 and 27:45.

15:34 Elo-i, Elo-i: Jesus quotes the opening line of Ps 22 in Aramaic (CCC 603, 2605). ● Psalm 22 forecasts both the Messiah's suffering and his eventual deliverance. The full context of Ps 22, in light of its hopeful outcome, rules out the possibility that Jesus succumbed to despair (Lk 23:46). See note on Mt 27:46.

15:38 the curtain: Two veils hung in the Jerusalem Temple to symbolize God's inaccessibility to sinners (Heb 9:8). One was visible, as it separated the outer courts from the sanctuary proper, and the other was invisible to all but the priests, as it hung inside the sanctuary in front of its most sacred chamber, the Holy of Holies (Ex 26:31–34; Heb 9:3, 7). Although the evangelist does not specify which of the two veils was torn, the lesson to be learned is clear: access to the Father is now open through Jesus, who as high priest has entered on our behalf (Eph 2:18; Heb 10:19–22). Moreover, as the curtain ripped **from top to bottom,** the barrier between the face of God and his people was removed, and the termination of the Old Covenant was prophetically announced. **was torn:** Mark uses the same Greek expression at 1:10 to describe God "tearing" the heavens at the Baptism of Jesus. If a connection is being made between these two events, as seems likely, it may have been the outer veil draped in front the sanctuary that was rent in two, since history (Josephus) testifies that it was embroidered with images of the cosmos.

15:39 centurion: A Roman commander of 100 soldiers. **Son**

---

[g] Other ancient authorities insert verse 28, *And the scripture was fulfilled which says, "He was reckoned with the transgressors"*.
[h] Or *earth*.

stood facing him, saw that he thus [i] breathed his last, he said, "Truly this man was the Son [x] of God!"

40 There were also women looking on from afar, among whom were Mary Mag´dalene, and Mary the mother of James the younger and of Joses, and Salo´me, [41]who, when he was in Galilee, followed him, and ministered to him; and also many other women who came up with him to Jerusalem.

The Burial of Jesus

42 And when evening had come, since it was the day of Preparation, that is, the day before the sabbath, [43]Joseph of Arimathe´a, a respected member of the council, who was also himself looking for the kingdom of God, took courage and went to Pilate, and asked for the body of Jesus. [44]And Pilate wondered if he were already dead; and summoning the centurion, he asked him whether he was already dead.[j] [45]And when he learned from the centurion that he was dead, he granted the body to Joseph. [46]And he bought a linen shroud, and taking him down, wrapped him in the linen shroud, and laid him in a tomb which had been hewn out of the rock; and he rolled a stone against the door of the tomb. [47]Mary Mag´dalene and Mary the mother of Joses saw where he was laid.

The Resurrection of Jesus

16 And when the sabbath was past, Mary Mag´dalene, and Mary the mother of James, and Salo´me, bought spices, so that they might go and anoint him. [2]And very early on the first day of the week they went to the tomb when the sun had risen. [3]And they were saying to one another, "Who will roll away the stone for us from the door of the tomb?" [4]And looking up, they saw that the stone was rolled back; for it was very large. [5]And entering the tomb, they saw a young man sitting on the right side, dressed in a white robe; and they were amazed. [6]And he said to them, "Do not be amazed; you seek Jesus of Nazareth, who was crucified. He has risen, he is not here; see the place where they laid him. [7]But go, tell his disciples and Peter that he is going before you to Galilee; there you will see him, as he told you." [8]And they went out and fled from the tomb; for trembling and astonishment had come upon them; and they said nothing to any one, for they were afraid.

Jesus Appears to Mary Magdalene

9 Now when he rose early on the first day of the week, he appeared first to Mary Mag´dalene, from whom he had cast out seven demons. [10]She went and told those who had been with him, as they mourned and wept. [11]But when they heard that he was alive and had been seen by her, they would not believe it.

Jesus Appears to Two Disciples

12 After this he appeared in another form to two of them, as they were walking into the country. [13]And they went back and told the rest, but they did not believe them.

Jesus Commissions the Disciples

14 Afterward he appeared to the eleven themselves as they sat at table; and he upbraided them for their unbelief and hardness of heart, because

---

15:40: Jn 19:25.   **15:41:** Lk 8:1–3.   **15:42–47:** Mt 27:57–61; Lk 23:50–56; Jn 19:38–42; Acts 13:29.   **15:42:** Deut 21:22–23.
16:1–8: Mt 28:1–8; Lk 24:1–10; Jn 20:1–2.   **16:1:** Lk 23:56; Jn 19:39.   **16:7:** Mk 14:28; Jn 21:1–23; Mt 28:7.

---

of God!: A confession of faith that stands in contrast to the taunting cries of the mob (15:14, 18, 29–30, 31, 32, 36). It marks a high point in Mark's Gospel, as it crowns the theme of Jesus' divine Sonship developed throughout (1:1, 11; 3:11; 9:7; CCC 444). It likewise adds more irony to Mark's narrative: a non-Jewish soldier was the only one to profess faith in the "King of the Jews" at the Cross (15:26). Similar faith is exhibited by a Gentile centurion in Mt 8:5–13 and Lk 7:1–10.

15:43 Joseph of Arimathea: A wealthy member of the Jewish Sanhedrin. According to Luke, he withheld his consent from the court's condemnation of Jesus (Lk 23:51). His courage as a "disciple of Jesus" (Jn 19:38) helped him to arrange the burial (Mt 27:57–60) and so risk his reputation as a respected leader in Israel. See note on 14:55.

15:46 in a tomb: Located in a garden near Jerusalem (Jn 19:41–42). The site had to be close by, since the Sabbath rest began at sunset and all labor would have to cease by then (15:42). See note on 1:21.

16:1–20 Easter morning marks the day of Christ's victory over death and the devil. Jesus himself foresaw this triumphant outcome of his Passion (8:31; 9:31; 10:34; 14:28).

16:1 the sabbath was past: It was after 6 P.M. on Holy Saturday. See note on 1:21.

16:2 first day of the week: Sunday morning. Christians commemorate this weekly as the "Lord's day" (Rev 1:10). It is a day

set apart for worship, rest, and the celebration of the Eucharist as an assembled Church (Acts 20:7; CCC 2174–77).

16:5 a young man: Matthew calls him an "angel of the Lord" (Mt 28:2).

16:6 He has risen: The Resurrection of Jesus is the greatest miracle of history. The NT describes it as a glorious accomplishment of the Trinity: the Father (Rom 6:4), Son (Jn 10:17–18), and Holy Spirit (Rom 1:4) were together active in bringing about Christ's Resurrection, glorification, and heavenly Ascension (CCC 648–50).

16:7 Peter: Simon is singled out as the leader of the apostolic band and the head of the New Covenant Church (Mt 16:17–19; CCC 642). The summons to meet Jesus indicates that Peter's cowardice has been forgiven (Lk 22:31–32). In John's Gospel, Peter three times affirms his love for Jesus as personal restitution for his threefold denial (Jn 21:15–17).

16:9–20 Ancient manuscripts of Mark's Gospel differ in their conclusions after 16:8. Two important fourth-century manuscripts simply end at 16:8. Other versions of Mark include a "short ending" of two sentences after 16:8. The majority of Marcan manuscripts, however, include this "longer ending" (16:9–20). According to the Council of Trent, the canon of Scripture corresponds to everything included in the Latin Vulgate edition (*Sess. 4, Dec. 1*). This official translation includes 16:9–20 as part of the inspired Gospel.

16:14 the eleven: Mark makes no mention of Judas Iscariot's suicide (Mt 27:3–5) but implies his elimination from the ranks of the Twelve (3:14; 14:10, 43).

---

[i] Other ancient authorities insert *cried out and*.   [x] Or *a son*.
[j] Other ancient authorities read *whether he had been some time dead.*

they had not believed those who saw him after he had risen. [15]And he said to them, "Go into all the world and preach the gospel to the whole creation. [16]He who believes and is baptized will be saved; but he who does not believe will be condemned. [17]And these signs will accompany those who believe: in my name they will cast out demons; they will speak in new tongues; [18]they will pick up serpents, and if they drink any deadly thing, it will not hurt them; they will lay their hands on the sick, and they will recover."

The Ascension of Jesus

19 So then the Lord Jesus, after he had spoken to them, was taken up into heaven, and sat down at the right hand of God. [20]And they went forth and preached everywhere, while the Lord worked with them and confirmed the message by the signs that attended it. Amen.[k]

16:15–16 Mark's account of the Great Commission stresses that the apostles must spread the Christian faith by (1) evangelization (**preach**) and (2) the administration of the sacraments (**baptized**; CCC 977, 1253, 1257). The apostles' mission to the **whole creation** includes all the nations of the world (Lk 24:47). See note on Mt 28:19.

16:17–18 The power of the gospel is displayed through the miracles of those who preach it. In the early Church, the apostles drove out **demons** (Acts 16:16–18), spoke in **new tongues** (Acts 2:4–11), sustained the sting of **serpents** un-

harmed (Acts 28:1–6), and healed infirmities by placing their **hands on the sick** (Acts 3:6–8; 28:8; CCC 434, 670). Although these signs are not ends in themselves, they can be motives of credibility that lead unbelievers to embrace the gospel and likewise lead believers to see the reasonableness of their faith.

16:19 taken up into heaven: Jesus ascended to heaven 40 days after his Resurrection (Acts 1:3). He is now enthroned as King and Judge at the Father's **right hand** (Col 3:1; Heb 12:2; CCC 659, 663). See note on 14:62.

---

[k] Other ancient authorities omit verses 9–20. Some ancient authorities conclude Mark instead with the following: *But they reported briefly to Peter and those with him all that they had been told. And after this, Jesus himself sent out by means of them, from east to west, the sacred and imperishable proclamation of eternal salvation.*

STUDY QUESTIONS

Chapter 1

For understanding
1. **1:4 Word Study: Repentance.** What does the Greek word *metanoia* mean? What does the New Testament use it to mean? If metanoia is a gradual process, how is it manifested?
2. **1:11.** What Old Testament passages does the Father's announcement that Jesus is "my beloved Son" echo? What do they say about Jesus' identity?
3. **1:12–13.** Though Mark provides few details of the temptation of Christ in the wilderness, what is the importance of some of the details he does provide, such as the presence of wild beasts, the leading into the desert by the Spirit, and the length of time spent there?
4. **1:44.** What is the reasoning behind Jesus' strategy of warning demons and men to keep silent about his identity?

For application
1. **1:6, 12–13.** Both John the Baptist and Jesus follow practices of self-discipline for religious reasons. What self-disciplinary practices do you use for religious (not health or other personal) reasons? How have they influenced your own "change of heart" (repentance)?
2. **1:7.** John the Baptist admits that he is not worthy to do even menial tasks for the Messiah. How does humility (the knowledge that you are not worthy of God) differ from feelings that you have no self-worth (self-loathing)? How does true humility enhance your self-worth in God's sight?
3. **1:20.** Zebedee's sons immediately left their father and his business to follow Jesus. How radical is your own response to his call? How rapid is it?
4. **1:35.** Jesus gets up well before daylight to pray in a remote spot. What do you imagine that the Son of God prayed about, and how might he have prayed? How frequently do you pray, and when, and where? What do you do when you pray?

Chapter 2

For understanding
1. **2:15–28.** This chapter outlines three controversies between the Pharisees and Jesus. What were they?
2. **Topical Essay: Who Are the Pharisees?** How does understanding the background of the Pharisees' quest for personal holiness cast the clashes between them and Jesus in a whole new light? What were the Pharisees trying to accomplish as opposed to what Jesus was trying to accomplish? In the end, if Jesus' conflicts with the Pharisees had little to do with disagreements over the Law, what did it have to do with?
3. **2:19.** Why is it inappropriate for Jesus' disciples to fast when the bridegroom is among them? Why do Christians fast before Communion?
4. **2:26.** Why does Jesus "mistakenly" refer to Abiathar as high priest in David's reign, when the high priest at the time was actually Ahimelech? What is the significance of Abiathar?

For application
1. **2:5.** Jesus responds to the faith of the paralytic's friends by forgiving the sick man's sins. As you reflect on your own life, how does sin tend to paralyze you spiritually? How does forgiveness of sin heal that paralysis?
2. **2:17.** Jesus has not come to call the righteous but sinners. In your heart of hearts, to which of the two classes do you think you belong? Do you really look on yourself as a sinner or as someone who is good?
3. **2:27.** What is your attitude toward the requirement to attend Mass on Sunday? What about the Church's prohibition of servile work? Do you see these requirements and prohibitions as making you fit the Sabbath or as a way of making the Sabbath for you?

Chapter 3

For understanding
1. **3:14.** What is the significance of the number of apostles Jesus appointed?
2. **3:22.** Who is Beelzebul to the scribes? Why did the scribes accuse Jesus of casting demons out by the power of Beelzebul?
3. **3:29.** If all sin can be forgiven in principle, why does Jesus refer to blasphemy against the Holy Spirit as an eternal sin? What sin in the Old Testament prefigures this sin?
4. **3:35.** What is the criterion Jesus gives for being his brother, sister, or mother? What then is his attitude to his biological mother, who has accompanied those relatives desirous of seizing him (v. 22)?

For application
1. **3:5.** What makes Jesus angry in this passage? What is there about your own life that might provoke this sort of anger in him?
2. **3:19b–21.** Why did Jesus' relatives think he was "beside himself"? Have you ever been criticized for "being too religious", or have you yourself criticized others for that? If either is the case, what do you think is the problem?
3. **3:24–27.** Who is the "strong man" in verse 27? If a "strong man" has gained a foothold in some area of your life, how can you bind him?
4. **3:31–34.** If you want to be a kinsman of Jesus, what will it take for you to be accepted as one?

Chapter 4

For understanding
1. **4:2.** How do Jesus' parables both conceal and reveal his message?
2. **4:11.** Why does Jesus explain the parables to his disciples but not to anyone else? According to the Second Vatican Council, what is Jesus ensuring in this way?
3. **4:30–32.** What does Jesus intend the parable of the Mustard Seed to depict? From what Old Testament imagery is his imagery drawn?
4. **4:35–41.** Why were the disciples "filled with awe" at Jesus' calming of the raging sea? What is the Old Testament background of this incident?

For application
1. **4:9.** How good are your spiritual ears? How do you hear the word of God? How do you know that you are hearing Jesus correctly?
2. **4:12.** How do you understand Jesus' use of irony in this passage? When you hear and understand what God is telling you, what kinds of changes in your life does his word entail? Does your understanding cause you to want to change or to ignore the message because you might need to change?
3. **4:13.** Jesus asks his disciples how they will understand any parable if they do not understand the parable of the Sower. As you listen to God's word for your life, what are the benchmarks you use for understanding? Where are you most likely to misunderstand?
4. **4:24–25.** How does this "use it or lose it" spiritual principle apply to your life?

Chapter 5

For understanding
1. **5:9.** Why is the name "Legion" significant for the spiritual state of the Gerasene demoniac? On an allegorical level, what does the demoniac represent?
2. **5:13.** How is the fate of the swine in the Gerasene incident like that of Pharaoh's army in Ex 14:26–28?
3. **5:21–43.** How are the two miracle stories in this passage linked?
4. **5:25.** Aside from the medical difficulties, what were the legal consequences of the woman's flow of blood? How does Jesus remove the problem?

For application
1. **5:15.** What do you think made the citizens of Gerasa afraid when they saw the former demoniac clothed and in his right mind? What has God done in your life or that of your family that has inspired a similar fear?
2. **5:18–19.** Why do you think Jesus refused to let the healed demoniac accompany him? Have you ever felt a desire to serve God that God did not seem to let you exercise? What came of it?
3. **5:25–28.** What attitude to Jesus' power does the woman with the flow of blood have, despite her experience with doctors? What can that attitude teach you about faith?
4. **5:36.** What does Jesus "ignore" in this passage? (Compare this approach with what he does in v. 40.) What does he tell the dead girl's father? What might God advise you to ignore in order to exercise faith?

Chapter 6

For understanding
1. **6:7–13.** According to St. Gregory the Great, what is the significance of sending the disciples out in pairs? What are the "twin precepts of charity"?
2. **6:23.** In what sense is the oath of Herod Antipas the mirror opposite of a similar scene in Esther 5:8, 7:1?
3. **6:35–44.** How does the miracle of the loaves look both backward and forward? What other passage in Mark uses the same sequence of verbs to describe Jesus' actions?
4. **6:41.** What is the significance of Jesus giving the multiplied loaves to the apostles to distribute?

For application
1. **6:1–6.** How does envy impede faith? Why does your envy at others' success keep Jesus from answering your prayers?
2. **6:30–32.** When was the last time you made a retreat? Why might Jesus invite you to make a retreat?
3. **6:34.** What was Jesus' reaction when he saw that his plans to take the apostles to a lonely spot for a rest were ruined by the crowds? What would be your reaction under similar circumstances? What does Jesus teach you here?
4. **6:50–51.** What does Jesus tell his disciples when they see him walking on the water? What does he do, and what happens next? What does Jesus say and do when the winds of contrary events rise in your life?

Chapter 7

For understanding

1. **7:11.** Why does Jesus condemn the contemporary practice of declaring one's personal possessions *Corban*, or dedicated to God?
2. **7:19.** In what two ways does Jesus set aside the distinctions between clean and unclean? What effect does his pronouncement have on the relationship between Jewish and Gentile Christians?
3. **7:21.** Why does Jesus place the source of defilement within the *heart* of a person rather than, say, the imagination?
4. **7:27.** Why does Jesus say that the children must be fed before the dogs when the Tyrian woman requests that he heal her daughter? What does the term "dog" indicate in this passage? What does the woman's reply reveal about her?

For application

1. **7:6-7.** How much of your prayer during the liturgy amounts to little more than lip service? How do you cope with distractions during Mass? What do you bring to the liturgy so as to draw your heart near to God?
2. **7:9-13.** How well do you obey the command to honor your parents? What do you do to show them honor? What practices (habits, family or social customs, religious duties, reactions to past events, or character traits) have impeded your duty to your parents?
3. **7:15-23.** Where is Jesus placing the responsibility for being clean—on the circumstances or on you? What events in your life might illustrate how things that come out of you make you clean or unclean?
4. **7:33.** Why do you think Jesus took the man aside to heal him in private? How has Jesus dealt privately with you (rather than treating you as part of a group)?

Chapter 8

For understanding

1. **8:6.** What is the significance of the Greek word used to translate "give thanks" in this verse?
2. **8:19-21.** What is the most probable view of the symbolism that underlies the two miracles of the loaves and the number of baskets collected in each?
3. **8:22-26.** Why does Jesus heal the blind man in stages? How does St. Jerome view the meaning of this passage?
4. **8:34.** How graphic is Jesus' use of imagery here to his audience? What does the image of "taking up one's cross" communicate to them?

For application

1. **8:17-18.** How have you failed to perceive or closed your mind to understanding what God is doing in your life? How have you heard Jesus' correction, and what have you done about it?
2. **8:26.** Compare the location of this miracle (Bethsaida) with what Jesus said about the town in Mt 11:21 and Lk 10:13. Why do you think that Jesus told the blind man, now healed, not to go into the village? How might Jesus want to separate you from your surroundings, and why?
3. **8:33.** Why would Jesus rebuke Peter upon seeing his (Jesus') disciples? How might your attitudes toward the ways God acts affect others?
4. **8:35.** In your experience, how can a person who wants to save his life actually lose it? How can a person who loses his life for the sake of Jesus actually save it? What do the verbs "saving" and "losing" mean in these paradoxes?

Chapter 9

For understanding
1. **9:1.** What did Jesus mean by saying that some among his hearers would not taste death before the coming of the kingdom of God? When will the coming of the kingdom be complete?
2. **9:11.** On what is the expectation of the "second coming" of Elijah based? What is the Old Testament context for the promise of Elijah's return?
3. **9:42–48.** Why does Jesus use hyperbole in connection with his remarks on avoiding sin? How does St. John Chrysostom view the meaning of these verses?
4. **9:43. Word Study: Hell.** Why does Jesus associate hell with Gehenna? What had happened there before Jesus' time? What was Gehenna used for in Jesus' day? What other scriptural passages underscore the horrifying nature of hell?

For application
1. **9:22–23.** How do you betray your lack of faith in God's power in your life?
2. **9:26–27.** What pattern of healing do you see in this passage? How might it apply to your life?
3. **9:35–37.** What does it mean for you to be "first of all" by being the "last of all"? In whose name must the little child be received? What kind of person would that "little child" be in your life?
4. **9:42–48.** What is your besetting weakness, the area where you are most likely to sin? What have you done to correct it? How do your efforts compare with the solutions Jesus suggests?

Chapter 10

For understanding
1. **10:6.** According to the passages in Genesis to which Jesus alludes, what are three characteristics of the marital bond? Why can it not be broken by any civil or religious authority?
2. **10:14.** What is the connection between Jesus' blessing of the children and the prohibition of divorce in vv. 11–12?
3. **10:38.** What is the "baptism" James and John are to be baptized with? What forms did that baptism take in their lives?
4. **10:45. Word Study: Ransom.** How is the concept of a ransom connected with family relations in the Old Testament? How does God in the Old Testament fulfill that family obligation? How does Jesus fulfill it in the New Testament?

For application
1. **10:1–12.** How might it be "hardness of heart" to use religious regulations to advance your own desires? How does the issue of divorce illustrate hardness of heart? How does acceptance of God's plan remove hardness of heart?
2. **10:22–27.** How many "possessions" do you have? How do they affect your relationship to Jesus? How dismayed are you when he asks you to give them up?
3. **10:35–40.** How does Jesus answer the prayer of his own disciples here? What can you learn about your own prayer when God's answer seems to be No?
4. **10:47.** What can you learn about prayer from the attitude and approach of the blind man Bartimaeus?

Chapter 11

For understanding
1. **11:8–10.** What three details surrounding the triumphal entry into Jerusalem recall Psalm 118?
2. **11:13.** Why does Jesus curse a fig tree when it is not even the season for figs?
3. **11:15.** What is the problem Jesus finds with the merchants in the court of the Gentiles, since selling sacrificial animals there is admittedly a service to pilgrims?
4. **11:17.** To which two passages from the Old Testament does Jesus' statement refer? How are both passages ultimately fulfilled?

For application
1. **11:1–6.** What is the most difficult or embarrassing thing Jesus has asked you to do? How have you responded to his request? What has been the outcome?
2. **11:9–10.** What echoes of the Mass do you find in these verses? If the word "Hosannah" is Hebrew for "Lord, save", would you have chosen that expression if you had been in the crowd celebrating Jesus' entry into Jerusalem? If not, what would you have shouted, and why?
3. **11:16.** What personal baggage do you "carry through the Temple area" when you come into it? Why do you think Jesus might forbid you to carry such baggage there?
4. **11:21–22ff.** Why do you think Jesus exhorts his disciples to "have faith in God" when Peter points out that the tree Jesus cursed has withered? Given the symbolism of the fig tree and Jesus' cursing of it, what is the connection with a living faith?

Chapter 12

For understanding
1. **12:1–9.** What two main points is the parable of the Wicked Tenants making? What do some of the details of the parable represent in the Jerusalem of Jesus' day?
2. **Topical Essay: Who Are the Sadducees?** How did the Sadducees originate? With what were they most closely associated? From what factors does the controversy surrounding the Sadducees come?
3. **12:26.** How does Jesus use Scripture to discuss the resurrection of the dead with the Sadducees? How can the text Jesus alludes to be considered a proof-text for them?
4. **12:36.** Using Psalm 110, Jesus asks the Pharisees how the Messiah, recognized by them to be the son of David, can be David's superior. From both the context of the psalm and theological reflection, how can the question Jesus asks be answered?

For application
1. **12:17.** What in your life belongs to "Caesar" (the state, your career, your secular or social commitments), and what belongs to God? In terms of the time you spend on each, how much of your life actually is given to God?
2. **12:26–27.** If God is the God not of the dead but of the living, what do you honestly believe about the fates of those you know who have died? What is your real opinion of what happens to you when you die? How does that compare with Church belief?
3. **12:34.** What do you think Jesus meant by telling the scribe that he was "not far" from the kingdom of heaven? Was Jesus commenting on his understanding of theology or his faith? What would he say of yours?
4. **12:41–44.** What is your approach to supporting the Church financially? What can you learn from Jesus' observation about the poor woman's contribution?

Chapter 13

For understanding
1. **13:14.** What is the "desolating sacrilege"? To what historical event does the expression refer?
2. **13:24-25.** How are we to understand Jesus' warnings about cosmic disturbances if the dramatic events he describes are not to be taken literally?
3. **13:30.** If the cosmic disturbances in vv. 24–25 are not to be taken literally, how do we understand Jesus' reference to "this generation"?
4. **13:35.** What are three levels of meaning to Jesus' command to be watchful?

For application
1. **13:5-7.** What events or persons exist in the modern world that can deceive Jesus' disciples regarding "the end"? What effect, if any, have they had on your own view of God's plan?
2. **13:13.** How hard is it for you to live your faith in your present circumstances? What does "persevering to the end" mean for you at this point in your life?
3. **13:32-37.** The need for watchfulness is greatest when the environment seems friendly but only gradually becomes hostile to faith, hope, or love—rather like boiling the proverbial frog by slowly turning up the heat. How has your social or religious environment worsened in ways that you may not have noticed? How have you been affected by the changes? What need of watchfulness do you see?

Chapter 14

For understanding
1. **14:22.** How does Jesus identify the unleavened bread of the Passover feast with his own flesh? What is the symbolism of breaking the unleavened bread?
2. **14:24.** What is the significance of the phrase "blood of the Covenant" that Jesus uses when he blesses the cup of wine?
3. **14:55.** What was the origin and primary role of the Sanhedrin? Who belonged to it? Under Roman rule, what could the Sanhedrin do? What could it not do?
4. **14:61. Word Study: Christ.** Why was the expected deliverer called an "anointed one"? What ministries was the Messiah supposed to have? What are some of the Old Testament references to the roles and fate of the Messiah?

For application
1. **14:7-9.** How important is it for you to minister to Jesus, according to this passage? Why do you think Jesus said that the woman's action would be told wherever the gospel is preached? What does her action teach you?
2. **14:32-42.** Have you ever faced a serious trial that you knew you could not avoid? What was it? How did you approach it? How similar was your approach to that of Jesus in the garden?
3. **14:38.** Even though the spirit of the apostles is "willing" (refer to v. 31), how did their weakness show itself? What are some examples in your own life of a similar willingness combined with similar weakness? What did you learn from it?
4. **14:66-72.** How do you respond to your failure to live up to your own expectations for holiness? What do you imagine God's attitude toward you is at those times? (What is it, really, regardless of how badly you feel about it?)

Chapter 15

For understanding
1. **15:11.** What is the irony in Barabbas' name? How does that contrast with the identity of Jesus?
2. **15:24.** Where did the practice of crucifixion come from? What caused death for a crucified person? What parallels did the early Christians see between the Crucifixion of Jesus and the fate of Adam?
3. **15:38.** What is the significance of the veil of the Temple? Why is its rending from top to bottom significant in view of the Jewish understanding of what the Temple stood for?
4. **15:39.** Why is the centurion's confession about Jesus the high point of Mark's Gospel?

For application
1. **15:10.** Mark says that the Jewish leaders handed Jesus over to Pilate "out of envy". Why would Mark choose that word rather than a more typical one, such as *malice*?
2. **15:33.** Read Wis 17 in connection with this passage. What might the darkness indicate? Why would episodes of sin in your life be described as "dark"?
3. **15:34.** Why do you think Jesus quotes Psalm 22? When you read the psalm, what do you notice about the way it ends? What might the ending suggest to you?

Chapter 16

For understanding
1. **16:6.** How do the Scripture passages listed in the note for this verse show that the Resurrection is a work of the Trinity?
2. **16:7.** What are two reasons Peter is singled out in this passage?
3. **16:9–20.** What is unusual about these verses in terms of the ancient manuscripts? Why does the Church regard them as part of inspired Scripture?
4. **16:15–16.** How does Mark's account of the great commission tell the apostles to spread the gospel?

For application
1. **16:6–8.** Why did the women not obey the "young man"? What about that experience would make them want to keep things quiet?
2. **16:11, 13.** According to the Catechism (CCC 643), the disciples' reaction of unbelief helps validate the historical nature of Jesus' Resurrection. How? What can you cite from your own experience that would explain how unbelief might confirm the truth of a claim?
3. **16:17–18, 20.** How does your experience of the Christian life square with the experience of the charisms mentioned here? If you have these charisms, or know of someone who does, what should these "signs" point to in your/their life?